The Shape of Zion

The Shape of
Zion

Leadership and Life
in Black Churches

Michael I. N. Dash
and Christine D. Chapman

Wipf & Stock
PUBLISHERS
Eugene, Oregon

In Memoriam
Jonathan Jackson
(1931–2002)
Colleague, scholar,
mentor, spiritual friend

Wipf and Stock Publishers
199 W 8th Ave, Suite 3
Eugene, OR 97401

The Shape of Zion
Leadership and Life in Black Churches
By Dash, Michael I. N. and Chapman, Christine D.
Copyright©2003 Pilgrim Press
ISBN 13: 978-1-55635-631-5
ISBN 10: 1-55635-631-5
Publication date: 8/3/2007
Previously published by Pilgrim Press, 2003

CONTENTS

6. Final Thoughts 130

Appendix A:
FACT Denominations and Faith Groups 167

Appendix B:
Denominational Charts of Rural-Urban-Suburban
Locations 169

Notes 177

Bibliography 183

Index 187

FOREWORD

At the end of the twentieth century and the beginning of the new millennium, some forty religious denominations, including Christian, Jewish, and Muslim groups, decided to complete a national survey of their congregations at the same time as the federal census of 2000. Faith Communities Today (FACT) represented the largest cooperative survey of different religious denominations ever undertaken. The Interdenominational Theological Center in Atlanta became the research base for the study of African American churches called Project 2000. One of the major concerns of the researchers was how to disseminate the results of the survey effectively to clergy and lay members of black church congregations and how to make statistical data understandable and helpful to them.

Michael Dash and Christine Chapman have succeeded admirably in fulfilling both goals in their book, *The Shape of Zion: Leadership and Life in Black Churches*. They have combined biblical and theological insights and concrete examples of congregations with the survey results in an effective manner. They have produced a highly readable resource guide that enables clergy and lay leaders to reflect upon aspects of their congregational life, compare them with national results, and work to improve them. Questions for discussion and self-evaluation are included at the end of each chapter.

This book is highly recommended to clergy, denominational and lay leaders, divinity students, and anyone interested in improving and transforming the congregational life of black churches, which still constitute the most important institutional sector of black communities across the country.

LAWRENCE H. MAMIYA
Paschall-Davis Professor of Religion
and Africana Studies at Vassar College
and co-author of *The Black Church
in the African American Experience*

PREFACE

Our first presentation of data from our research was to a group of national Baptist leaders. Each of them was a distinguished leader of a local congregation that was engaged in exciting ministries. All of them had spent numerous years responding to the needs of people in their communities. Their many ministries were expressions of faithful, obedient, and extremely effective service. One pastor's statement to us at the conclusion of our presentation was, "Now that you have shown us what we look like and some areas where our congregation life could be enhanced, and shown us some challenges we face, what solutions have you got for us?" Was it a trick question, or was it a sincere appeal for help? We suspect it was the latter.

This is a practical and functional resource book that presents ways for self-evaluation and analysis of religious congregations. Our research produced rich data on the black church in America at the start of a new millennium. Now we need to provide principles and guidance for religious leaders as practical application for the findings. This book invites serious reflection and encourages you to engage in creative imagination of new and different possibilities for congregational life in all its varied dimensions. It challenges you to explore and find ways for achieving a future for your congregation that only you can envision.

It is our hope that you who read our book may not only discover what is the shape of your congregation but explore ways in which you might contribute to that life and effect any necessary transformation.

Each of us brought to this task a variety of interests and gifts that have been enhanced through our relationships with pastors and people in several congregations. We are thankful for their generous sharing and gracious hospitality. We celebrate the dedication and devotion of pastors and members in those congregations to be the people of God in their fellowship and in their communities. Our several meetings with the faithful have enriched our understanding of the shape of congregational life. These associations and affiliations have helped and inspired us in our attempts through this book to encourage and challenge you as you examine the life of your congregation. We have discovered, as we hope you will, that the process can enrich your life as you seek to be more faithful and obedient to your vocation under God.

We are grateful to many persons in our community at the Interdenominational Theological Center who have provided support services in a variety of ways as we have engaged in this project. Special thanks in this regard are due to Melody Berry, CeCe Dixon, and Mary Larché.

We are able to bring this manuscript to publication because of Reta L. Bigham, who was our copy editor. She brought to the task her knowledge, expertise, and professionalism. These were complemented by her faithful commitment both to the assignment and to us.

We would like to express deep gratitude and appreciation to all our colleagues at ITC, especially those who have been our conversation partners: Steve Rasor, Ed Smith, and Marsha Haney, our fellows in the Institute for Black Religious Life (IBRL). In both formal and incidental encounters, we benefited from their scholarship. Writing a book while teaching full time and completing a doctoral dissertation is not an easy task. We appreciate the enthusiastic support, knowledge and wisdom of all our colleagues. They also shared with us their varied experiences and passion for congregations and persons who seek deeper relationship with God in those faith communities. We also honor the memory of the late Jonathan Jackson, one of our colleagues and mentors. His death occurred while we were writing this book. In our grief, we celebrate his life. His life touched and inspired us in many special ways as he journeyed among us in the ITC community.

We also mention and thank Mary Anne Bellinger, Douglas Ealey, and Renita Thomas, who listened to our ideas and offered thoughtful insights and suggestions. However, the shape of our work and the ultimate responsibility for the perspectives presented are our own.

Finally, each of us is grateful to members of our immediate families. We could not have persevered without unwavering love, support, and encouragement from those we cherish: Linda, Jan, Ginneh, Richard, Michelle, and Nathaniel; Steve, Leah, Alianor, Max, and Zack. This book is a small offering to them for love, patience, respect, and selfless and committed support.

PROJECT 2000 AND BEYOND THE NATIONAL PROFILE

One thing I asked of the LORD, that I will seek after: to live in the house of the LORD all the days of my life, to behold the beauty of the LORD, and to inquire in his temple.

—Psalm 27:4

GOD'S MINUTE

I have only one minute
only sixty seconds in it
forced upon me, can't refuse it
didn't seek it, didn't choose it;
It's up to me to use it,
I will suffer if I lose it, must give account
if I abuse it,
just a tiny minute, but...
eternity is in it.

—Benjamin E. Mays

The verse from Psalm 27 quoted above is a statement of confidence. It expresses the absolute certainty that, regardless of any threat, confidence is based on God. This verse is one of the most single-minded statements of purpose in the Hebrew Scriptures. The central point is requesting permission to live permanently in God's

1

presence. Although the psalm should not be taken literally (after all, one could not live permanently in a church or temple), it does refer to living always within God's presence. It is faith in God, renewed in the place that is the house of God, that contributes to fearlessness in the face of threats.

An elemental bond of group identity is belonging to a religious community. For African Americans, the church has long played a role of sanctuary. Social conditions placed a special burden on black churches; they had to be social centers, political forums, schoolhouses, mutual aid societies, refuges from racism and violence, and places of worship. Most African societies view humans as living in a religious universe.[1] Thus, natural phenomena, objects, and all of life are associated with acts of God, and religious beliefs, symbols, and rituals often define communities. Most African Americans have adopted and adapted Christian, chiefly Protestant, traditions to mark their place on the pluralistic American landscape. Exact statistics are difficult to gather, but about seventeen million members belong to the seven largest U.S. black denominations, representing the Methodist, Baptist, and Pentecostal-Holiness connections.[2] As we enter a new millennium, Project 2000 recorded ways in which the ongoing process of congregational life is lived in the United States.

This introduction discusses the following:

- the national survey of religion in the United States

- findings from ITC/FaithFactor Project 2000

- challenges of pastoral leadership

- the benefits of reading this book

- the structure of the book

- how to get the most from this book

The National Survey

In 2000 the nation's largest survey of U.S. congregations was conducted. It was an inclusive, denominationally sanctioned analysis meant to provide a public profile of American congregations. The project was initiated in the early 1990s as the Cooperative Congregational Studies Project (CCSP). FACT (Faith Communities Today), a research and educational program based at Hartford Seminary in Connecticut, managed the project. Project participants developed a common core questionnaire that was then adapted to represent individual faith traditions. Adaptations of the core questionnaire incorporated changes related to the use of words and phrases associated with individual traditions — for example, using minister, priest, rabbi, imam, and so on, where appropriate.

Forty-one denominations and faith groups participated in the national survey (see appendix A). The largest faith groups participating in the national study were historically black Protestant denominations. ITC/FaithFactor Project 2000 contributed to the national project by surveying historically black Protestant denominations. These included African Methodist Episcopal (AME), African Methodist Episcopal Zion (AMEZ), Christian Methodist Episcopal (CME), Church of God in Christ (COGIC), National Baptist Convention, Progressive National Baptist Convention, and black congregations within the Presbyterian Church USA and the United Methodist Church.

The ITC/FaithFactor Project 2000

Background to the Project

In the fall of 1998, Carl Dudley of the Hartford Institute for Religious Research and Lawrence Mamiya of Vassar College visited us at the Interdenominational Theological Center (ITC) with an invitation to assist them in the Cooperative Congregational Studies

Project (CSSP). ITC's specific task was to gather data on historically black denominations. Larry Mamiya spent a sabbatical year with us on the project assisting us as lead researcher. His expertise of more than three decades in the field of African American congregational studies and particularly his work with the renowned C. Eric Lincoln were most useful to us. Two ITC faculty members, Michael I. N. Dash and Stephen C. Rasor, directed Project 2000. Our initial response after committing to the project was to solicit the support of the six denominational deans within ITC.

ITC is a consortium of six denominations, and their presence is represented and supported by the denominational deans. When we explained the project to the deans, they were excited about the opportunity to participate in it. The deans assisted us in the provision of limited lists of pastors in their denominations, provided leadership on the Project 2000 Advisory Board, and were instrumental in disseminating the findings of the study throughout their denominations. Since there is a distinct lack of availability of records that reflect numbers of churches and pastors in individual denominations, we also used a list of churches and church leaders that was provided by Tri-Media. This list reflected those churches and pastors who have ordered materials for Sunday school purposes.

The ITC then engaged the Gallup Organization to assist in gathering the data. In our consultations with colleagues at Gallup, we agreed that for maximum response, telephone interviews would be most beneficial. The Gallup Organization has a well known and acclaimed record with this methodology.

Gallup conducted the telephone surveys between February 22 and May 11, 2000. A total of 1,863 senior pastors or lay leaders of black or predominantly black churches were interviewed. The average telephone interview was sixteen minutes in length. An initial question, designed as a screening mechanism, sought to gain the cooperation of the pastor. The screening process also included a confirmation of the denomination. If the pastor was not available during the field period, Gallup interviewed the church's assistant pastor or senior lay leader. Of the total of 1,863 interviews, 1,482 (77 percent) were conducted with the pastor while 381 (23 percent) were conducted with the assistant pastor or senior lay leader.[3] It must be noted that the sample of 1,863 persons represented the largest number of surveys for any one group in the total national sample.[4] The following is a denominational breakdown of the total number of completed interviews:

Total number of interviews	1,863
Church of God in Christ (COGIC)	503
Baptist	502
Christian Methodist Episcopal (CME)	295
African Methodist Episcopal (AME)	257
African Methodist Episcopal Zion (AMEZ)	110
Black Presbyterian	101
Black United Methodist	95

The persons conducting telephone surveys interviewed black church officials concerning key areas of congregational life. They gathered relevant data about sermons, worship patterns, community service, sources of conflict, financial health, and key demographic characteristics of the pastors and their congregants.

In addition to participation in the national congregational study, as reported by the Faith Communities Today project, we conducted additional research on black megachurches and urban storefront churches as a part of the Project 2000 study. This book reflects the reality of local and national African American congregations in the United States at the turn of a new century. It is designed to help religious leaders to respond effectively to the needs of their people through self-evaluative discovery of their identity as a community of faith.

Some Findings from Project 2000

Project 2000 enables local pastors, denominational officials, and congregational leaders to understand what congregations are doing regarding worship, spiritual growth, community outreach, managing, and leading. Although all of the findings of Project 2000 will be discussed in detail throughout, there are several key facts we uncovered and confirmed about the black churches. Some of these truths are that these churches emphasize:

- leadership with clarity of purpose
- diversity of church music
- incorporation of new members
- commitment to social justice
- numerous community outreach services
- financial stability

But beyond the facts, the history, and community contributions, congregations are also important for their purely religious significance. While most religious traditions emphasize the importance of community as the place where God is worshiped, within African American life, one of the strongest forces is a deep sense of relatedness. Religion, understood as being one with life, is not an isolated part of the community's life, but permeates every facet of the community's existence.[5] This book takes congregational life seriously. We invite you to consider carefully the nature of congregational life and to explore congregational identity as a community of faith in your location.

The Challenges of Pastoral Leadership

Religious organizations want to know more about congregations and the communities they serve. These faith groups want to learn what their congregations are like, how they worship, and how they function. They want to discover how their congregations can address the needs of their members and their neighborhoods.

Today we call on our religious leaders to have answers, make decisions, possess strength of character, offer a map of the future, and be persons who know where they ought to be going — in short, we want them to make hard problems simple. Being a religious leader has always required a unique set of leadership skills and talents. Leaders do not have easy answers to the challenges faced each day by most of their constituents, their congregants, and people in their communities.

More and more, religious leaders face increasing challenges: how to serve the people within their churches spiritually; how to serve the needs of people in their communities; and how to effectuate long-term societal changes. These issues are both a burden and a challenge to pastoral leadership. It is the goal of this book to give religious leaders tools with which to reflect on and address some of these challenges. While this is not a book about leadership or social change, it does give important information about the strengths of the black church in America and the role of the church today. This book also provides principles and guidelines for church leaders who are responsible for developing programs and ministries internal and external to their churches.

Leadership shapes congregational life. But congregational life is also shaped by the way a congregation is led to examine how conversation about a common life is shared, how a vision is articulated and owned by the congregation, how a communal investment is made to become people of God in context and time, and how a mission for faithful and obedient engagement can be pursued. No one pastor could respond to all these challenges and effect necessary changes. Many influential people who bring their professional and personal skills share leadership in the work that helps to shape life within the congregation.

The Benefits of Reading
This Book

This resource book is written to help the leaders, both pastors and
laypersons, improve the capacity of their congregations for engaging in meaningful ministry. While the approach and process design
here will serve a wide range of churches, the book is written with
small-to-medium-size congregations (those with few and moderate
resources) particularly in mind.

Pastors often find themselves caught up in the myth of leadership.
The myth goes something like this: the leader is a solitary individual whose brilliance enables her or him to lead the way. From the
perspective of the pastor who leads with this type of authority, constituents sometimes confer power in exchange for being relieved of
problems.

Effective pastors today are challenged to give the work of congregational development back to people without abandoning them.
This book was written as a resource for both pastors and congregational leaders to help them to effectively work together informally
or as educational committees within their congregations with the
goal of fostering congregational development.

Finally, ministerial students who are studying congregational life
as part of their theological education and preparation for ministry
will appreciate having this resource that brings together theology
and the practice of ministry.

Chapter-by-Chapter
Overview

We have organized the chapters of this volume around the five
broad areas used to conduct Project 2000:

- worship and identity
- facilities

- internal and mission-oriented programs
- leadership and organizational dynamics
- finances

Each chapter offers basic information, meaningful graphs, and guidelines and procedures for examining congregational life, its meaning, purpose, and potential. Questions for discussion, reflection, and action, and resources for further study will close each chapter.

Chapter 1 examines four aspects of congregational life related to dynamic worship and identity: spiritual vitality, music, preaching, and assimilation of new members.

Chapter 2 discusses congregational size, space, and facilities. Distribution of churches by region, rural-urban location, congregational size, size of churches and types of community, the year congregations were organized and characteristics of actively participating congregations are discussed.

Chapter 3 presents concepts and techniques for the practice of ministry. Participation in religious and social programs is discussed to provide crucial information on important internal and mission-oriented programs. Considerations related to participation in civil rights issues and interactions with significant relational groups are used to highlight ways congregations develop awareness and appreciation of their cultural underpinnings.

Chapter 4 addresses important issues of leadership and organizational dynamics related to having a spiritually vital congregation. In this chapter denominational heritage and the role of women pastors are highlighted.

Chapter 5 explores several aspects of church financial health. Topics discussed include financial health, church size and growth, as well as financial health and proportion of low-income families in the congregation.

Finally, chapter 6 offers models and detailed suggestions for developing an assessment in relation to other congregations, making fundamental decisions for the future, identifying strengths, and developing strategic objectives.

Throughout, illustrations and examples from real-life congregations that are applying the concepts discussed are offered. Also, each chapter concludes with a series of questions that you might ponder on your own or discuss within your congregation as one way of developing interest in discovering your congregational identity as a community of faith and making decisions about a desired future.

How to Get the Most from This Book

The black church has been at the center of the academic, political, and civic leadership that has served the black community in the United States. More than 80 percent of blacks in the United States regard religion and faith as very important to their personal lives.[6] How and where people practice their faith journeys is thus important. Congregations provide influence and support to both the individuals who belong to them and the communities where they are located.[7] They provide significant opportunities for gathering, communities of friendship and mutual support, spaces in which people can voice their discontents, and organizations through which they can mobilize for action. Andrew Billingsley writes:

> If we are to understand the sources and resources of the survival, achievements, and regeneration of the African American people and their communities, we would do well to consider the churches. They stand to represent the deep well of spirituality that keeps these people going. They are enormously resourceful and potent agents of social reform.

Their contributions to past, present, and future are not well understood or appreciated by many black and white Americans and others as well. They are misunderstood not only among the skeptics but among the believers as well; not only among the laity but among the priestly class as well; and not only among scholars and leaders and professionals but among laypeople as well.[8]

This book provides guidance for church leaders to engage their congregations in meaningful ministry. It is designed to help pastors and leaders of congregations discover the meaning, purpose, and potential of their congregations. Readers will find that it brings together theology and practice of ministry within a framework that will

- develop interest in discovering their identity as a community of faith;
- improve capacity of engaging in meaningful ministry;
- identify resources available to them; and
- offer questions for discussion, reflection, and action.

The material can be studied systematically from beginning to end, or readers can consult chapters topically as in a reference book.

Some Questions to Consider for Church Leaders

This book is an invitation for readers along with others to engage in a reflective and meaningful exploration of congregational identity. It is an invitation, for instance, to pastors of congregations (and ministerial students studying to become pastors) to think of congregations as places where meaningful ministry can be discovered and where the practice of community can be examined. General questions that might be considered include

- How do we help our congregations prioritize church programming?
- What are our presuppositions in terms of worship, liturgy, and music?
- What does social justice mean in church, society, and world?

Most important, this is also an invitation to people who populate and lead congregations to discover their identity as faith communities engaging in ministry. This book hopefully will bring together spirituality and the practice of ministry to improve the work God is calling them to do.

This is not an answer book, prescribing solutions to problems identified and challenges being encountered. It is a resource book that offers ways for you to engage in self-evaluation and analysis of the congregation in which you are involved. It also invites serious reflection and encourages you to engage in creative imagination of new and different possibilities for congregational life in its varied dimensions. It challenges you to explore and find ways for achieving a future that you envision.

Checklist for the Introduction

- Congregational development
- Discovering a framework for ministry
- Congregational evaluation

Questions for Discussion, Reflection, and Action

1. What are clear theological tenets that guide the mission and ministry of your congregation?
2. In what ways does a theological framework shape the thinking, work, and life of your congregation?

3. What opportunities and occasions exist for conversation about God in your congregation?

4. Are there care groups in your congregation where persons develop supportive, open, healing, and trusting relationships with others in which all experience and express the love of God in Jesus Christ?

~ *One* ~

DIMENSIONS OF CONGREGATIONAL LIFE

Day by day as they spent much time together in the temple, they broke bread at home and ate their food with glad and generous hearts, praising God and having the goodwill of all the people. And day by day the Lord added to their number those who were being saved.　　　　—Acts 2:46–47

Let there be a congregation which is careless of maintaining its fellowship, and we shall find it soon ceases to be a community engaged in meaningful service, in service that bears testimony to Jesus as Lord.　　　　—D. T. Niles

In this chapter you will learn about

- congregational culture
- dynamic worship and inspiring music
- the content and quality of preaching
- assimilation of new members

That brief glimpse into a window on the life of the early church in Acts describes a new kind of community, marked by fellowship, joyous worship, and a commitment to the welfare of all persons. Although the church is a human institution where people gather together, speak, eat, and sing, it is more than what human beings do. Indeed, the church finds its origin in the mighty deeds of God in Jesus Christ and the dynamic explosion of the Spirit's power symbolized by a mighty wind, tongues of fire, and the miracle of language. At the end of the story Luke tells us "day by day the Lord added to their number those who were being saved."

There is a connection between bringing men and women into a personal relationship with Jesus Christ and responsible church membership. The care of members within the community of the congregation — how persons are accepted and find mutual support — is reflected in the way a congregation lives out its mission and ministry. There are concrete signs between inner vitality and community outreach.

D. T. Niles tells how he had made a new discovery while on a visit to the United States. The word "fellowship" was a verb and not a noun, so here in the United States we talk of "fellowshipping" with one another. Niles writes:

> In the New Testament, fellowship is a noun which comes down from heaven. The early disciples found that they were in fellowship — Jew and Gentile, Greek and barbarian, bondsman and freeman, male and female. By themselves they could not achieve it, often they did not want it, but simply found that it was given to them and that they were under compulsion to maintain it and live by it. Today, when we fellowship with one another, we seek out people we like because they hold the same theology, or belong to the same class, or have the right color. The result is not a Church but a mutual admiration society. We need to learn again from the New Testament to seek and receive that fellowship which comes as a gift and a compulsion, remembering that where this is missing even worship and sacraments lose their meaning.[1]

Congregational Culture

A Christian congregation is a gathered community of faith with a story. God calls persons into community. The church is the called-out community. That is one meaning of the Greek word *ecclesia* — the community of persons who have responded to the call of God to a life together. The church is also apostolic by its very nature. The church is the people of God called out of the "world" but also sent back into the world to witness to the gospel. The good news of God's love is for all persons over the whole inhabited earth. Life in the congregation is the story of individuals and members as a group who are discovering and sharing life together and seeking to witness to that life under God in Jesus Christ. Indeed the ordered life in the community of faith is preparation for the life of mission in and to the world.

Life in a congregation is the story of persons who are engaged together in a journey and adventure with God and under the guidance of God's Spirit. It is a story of relationship and interaction. One might illustrate or view it as a cyclical process of discovery and sharing: *my story, your story,* and *our story* with God in a particular place. Everyone contributes to the story out of his or her giftedness. That is, God, who makes a diversity of gifts available to everyone, has gifted every person. No one who has had or claims to have had an encounter with God comes empty-handed to a congregation or faith community, whatever the nature or level of that encounter. Each person contributes to community life and can have a "piece of the action."

Difference as Strength

The group of leaders in one local church had gathered to discuss the national profile in relation to the understanding of the shape of life in their congregation. Their discussion was very animated. They confessed in a report in the plenary that in some instances, even though they were looking at the same question, they had different perspectives. This is the reality as we look at congregational life. Persons bring who they are in the totality of their being to life and to this interaction in the community of faith. This fact should be affirmed, and members should be encouraged to embrace the notion that strength exists in their diversity. Within the Christian community, difference is an occasion for celebration. This freedom will maximize the investment and participation of all members of the community.

In Ephesians 4:7–16 Paul offers some insights into congregational life. The congregation is a community called into being by God in Jesus Christ and is the family of God in heaven and on earth. That is the meaning of our profession in the communion of saints. Persons are by their baptism called to belong to the one body of Jesus Christ. Each member is grace-gifted by Jesus Christ, who has made different gifts available to each of us according to his grace. The responsibility of the church is to enable members to discover and develop their gifts for the sake of ministry in the world. It is through engagement in the ministry that each of us shares and grows together to maturity. The measurement for that maturity is not in our relationship to one another, but in how we measure up to the stature of Jesus Christ. We bring our several gifts to the task, and Jesus Christ uses all of them.

How We Do Things Here

William Watley told the story of how when he arrived at a new church, he discovered an interesting practice.[2] The head usher would stand up in front of the church, near the chancel, holding a big offering plate. Watley's mother, who had been visiting, asked him why the head usher stood in that position. He declared that he did not know; he'd only been at that church for three years. To his surprise, she chastised him, stating that since he was the pastor, he ought to know and that if he didn't, he ought to find out. He attempted to find out by asking the head usher, who had been serving in that position for the last twenty-five years! The brother took offense that he should be questioned in the matter. After Watley affirmed the head usher in his role and faithful service over this long period, the brother said that Brother Reid had held the position for an equal amount of time as the head usher, and when Brother Reid died, the board gave the new usher the responsibility and he had been in service ever since, doing things exactly as Brother Reid had. There were other usher boards in the church, and Watley sought to receive the answer to "why" from them. Their contention was that since the first usher board had done things that way, they were only following suit. He thereafter called all the usher boards together and gave them a month to return with a reason for the practice. Somebody came back with the answer that when the head ushers were up there they didn't know what to do with their hands. Sometimes they would be scratching here, pulling stuff down there; some were putting their hands in their pockets; so they gave them this plate to hold. Hence a practice was begun. Its origin was lost in memory until the new pastor's mother inquired. The book *Studying Congregations* states:

> Culture is who we are and the world we have created to live in. It is the predictable patterns of who does what and habitual strategies for telling the world about the things held most dear.... [It] ... includes the congregation's history and stories of its heroes. It includes the symbols, rituals, and worldview. It is shaped by the cultures in which its members live (represented by their demographic characteristics), but it takes on its own unique identity and character when those members come together.[3]

Discussions about the congregation's culture usually invite explorations into three levels of its life: church artifacts, values, and stories. Artifacts are generally understood as those objects that adorn selected and sacred spaces and those relationships and behaviors that are pursued by persons in the congregation. The values that members share help to shape their responses to various situations, persons, and contexts. The stories that people tell about traditions held present a picture of who they have been, who they are, or even who they think they are and who they hope to be. The myths they cherish are also very much a part of a congregation's culture.

There is a link between culture and identity. The identity of each congregation is shaped by history, circumstance, and doctrine. Further, these distinctions are reflected in ethnicity, location, and culture. Each congregation acts out of its self-understanding. Any other action is inauthentic. Congregations that do not pursue activities from this perspective seek to be like others. Interesting and useful ministry may arise from that community of faith, but no deep and meaningful engagement that expresses faithfulness and obedience to their calling as people of God. Persons in congregations need to be assisted to affirm and accept themselves for who they are. Even though each congregation has similarities with others, each is also unique. That uniqueness is found in its history, the personalities that are in fellowship there, and the context or location in which it is situated.

From the national profile of congregational life of different faiths in the United States, "sociologists report that denomination is declining in significance for congregational identity.... One also finds that the expression of denominational heritage tends to be stronger in those congregations with a distinctive racial/ethnic/national identity."[4] These facts remind us that local congregations are bearers of larger and national traditions within denominations.

Nearly three decades ago, Andrew Greeley wrote a book titled *The Denominational Society: A Sociological Approach to Religion in America.*[5] In that very interesting study, Greeley proposes that denominationalism was a central characteristic of American religion. No established church or religious body is sanctioned by the state. There is religious pluralism, and the several denominations provide not only meaning for the devotees, but also a place in which ethnic groups can bond with one another. The denominations reflect practices and styles of church life, and differences are also observable in their belief systems. In time, denominational heritage has helped create bonds among members and deepened spirituality and vitality of congregational life.

Denominational traditions are important influences shaping the ethos and identity of the congregation. These traditions include special emphases and distinctive styles of worship and practice. Baptist preparation for the regular worship service includes a session led by deacons. The platform worship leaders in the AME church fall down on one knee, holding on to the pulpit as the invocation is offered. Members of the Church of God in Christ have a session of praise at the beginning of worship, as they put their hands together for God and affirm, "This is the day / this is the day that the Lord has made." These examples are offered merely to suggest how denominational heritage impacts congregational culture.

Theological Reflection and Faith Development

We have rediscovered that doing theology is no longer the exclusive privilege of those who have a seminary education. Everyone who professes to have had an encounter with God in Jesus Christ and talks about ways in which that encounter affects their daily life is doing theology. Part of the congregation's story is the collective sharing of these separate encounters with God and the explorations into meaning and the discovery of challenges that those understandings present for individuals and the community.

Conversation in the community of faith may occur at different levels and in varied ways. Conversation always happens whenever and wherever people gather — in the fellowship hall, after the worship service in the narthex and in the parking lot. "Conversation is different from discussion and argument. It is less pointed and focused. In its early history, the word converse meant not only to talk, but also to live and dwell, and was sometimes also used to mean sexual intercourse."[6] Yet the essence of conversation is talking with one another, and not just talking. Conversation involves exchange — exchange of words and ideas. It involves speaking and listening to one another. But so often, we like to speak, to be heard, to hear ourselves, and we are hesitant, or reluctant, to listen to others as they share their words, their ideas.

Good and productive conversation demands good listening skills. It requires the hearer suspend the anxiety bubbling within as we concentrate on what we wish to say by way of response. And if we don't stay with the external conversation, we will miss the opportunity for appropriate response. These exercises of conversation in the congregation can be developed as a means of helping persons to talk and share their faith, exploring ways in which we can discover and draw from one another as we proceed on our Christian journey.

The Bible as Source Book for the Christian Faith

Gustavo Gutiérrez in an extremely interesting study of the book of Job contends that "central to the book itself is the question of *how we are to talk about God*. More particularly, how we are to talk about God from within a specific situation — namely, the suffering of the innocent."[7] That kind of testimony is not exclusive to Job. But can we talk about God when we go down, down, down to the depths until, as we express it in the African American tradition, "down don't bother no mo'e," when sorrows like sea billows roll, when pain lingers on and on and on and seems unending, when the heart becomes heavy and rent with grief, when a loved one is, as it were, snatched from us, suddenly, or when after a long and protracted illness that loved one wastes away and dies? How do we talk about God? How do you talk about God? How do you talk to God?

The Bible is the story of relationship between God and human beings, our encounter and interaction with one another. We meet God in the Bible. As we seek to understand God there, we will learn to find God in the world in which we live today. The Bible is both the Word in a particular historical situation and also the Word for us today. If we are to talk about God, we need to meditate and reflect on that relationship and discern the ways that God is working in our lives, the claims that God is making upon us, and the response that we are offering in faithfulness and obedience.

Someone has suggested that biblical knowledge and thinking get left on the stage once the diploma is received and commencement ends. For all the education they receive, seminary graduates continue to leave members in congregations at the level of their Sunday school experience. We are called to love God "with all your heart and with all your soul, and with all your mind and with all your strength" (Mark 12:30; cf. Deut. 6:5). Bible study involves more than textual analysis and reflection on meaning. We are invited to discern what decisions are right and what actions are necessary. The effect on our minds must be matched with feet that walk in the way of the Lord. Both the Hebrew and the Christian Scriptures emphasize covenant relationship in community. It is in communion with one another that we not only come face to face with the biblical message, but also discover our responsibility to keep covenant with God and others in community.

Dynamic Worship, Inspiring Music

On a visit to a local church, we arrived for 11:00 a.m. about five minutes after the hour. The worship service had already started. Many of our fellow worshipers were also arriving at that time. The ushers guarding the door were strict in the observance of entry protocols. It was praise time. There was no admittance at that juncture. The praise session went on until 11:20. Kinetic energy was infused into the experience, fueled by a procession of incessant tambourines — "to glory!"

The session was supported by the usual piano and organ, complemented by bass guitar and drums. The musicians vied to outdo one another in expressiveness, reminiscent of African dance exercises.

After the pastoral prayer, there was a selection by the chorus. A lot of times the music was so loud that the words were difficult to understand. Were we responding and just interested in a feeling and a good performance? We strained to hear, yet throughout the sanctuary persons got up in affirmation. Some meaning must have emerged as persons started to gesture, with their left and right hands alternately. Maybe one needs to be tuned in, to listen with the inner ear.

We are accustomed to so much constant activity in our worship services that any suggestion for a period of silence can be viewed as severe discipline. Yet such a pause in the flow of the worship has possibilities for creating space to listen and be tuned in to hear the voice of God. If we are to hear what God has to say, we must listen. Within the worship experience, God speaks to us as we prepare to worship. We must listen so that we might bring ourselves fully into God's presence. We must listen so that we might hear the Word proclaimed in the reading of the Scriptures and in the preaching. We must also find a place to be silent and listen after the preaching so that we may discern and decide ways of obedience to God. In Psalm 62:5 the psalmist is perhaps preparing to make a pilgrimage, so he confesses, "For God alone my soul waits in silence." It is that silence that creates a space for revelation. It is from the session of silence and contemplation that an authentic spirituality arises and invites a commitment to life.

In the African American experience each historical era and its experience have helped this particular people to tell their story. In

Africa and in parts of the African Diaspora, songs emerged in the contexts of celebrations and festivals. Those songs always included some praise to the Supreme Being or God. In the slave period, the "sorrow" songs were forged out of the crucible of pain and suffering. For the slave ancestors those songs were affirmations of God, sustaining a people in spite of the brutality and dehumanization that they experienced. Through those spirituals, slaves sang of a hope that "trouble don't last always." It is the biblical hope that the psalmist expressed after raising questions about relationship with God that evoked praise (Ps. 42:11; 43:3–4).

William McClain reminds us:

> Worship in the black tradition is celebration of the power to survive and to affirm life, with all of its complex and contradictory realities. The sacred and the secular, Saturday night and Sunday morning, come together to affirm God's wholeness, the unity of life and his lordship over all of life. Such a tradition encourages responses of spontaneity and improvisation, and urges worshipers to turn themselves loose into the hands of the existential here and now where joy and travail mingle together as part of the reality of God's creation. It is in this context that black people experience the life of faith and participate in the community of faith.[8]

Music has always been an important element in most worship services. Slightly more than half the pastors report that spirituals are "always" included in their services (52 percent). Wide differences, as might be expected, are noted across denominational lines. Over one-half of Baptists, COGIC, and CME clergy state that they always include spirituals in their services; only 21 percent of black Presbyterians and 30 percent of black United Methodists report this. Some differences emerge on the basis of educational background.[9]

Mellonee Burnim writes:

Negro spirituals and gospel music are the two indigenous musical genres that have historically dominated the worship of black Americans in the United States. . . . Negro spirituals and gospel music are the religious music genres actually created *by* and *for* Black people by themselves and which therefore reflect African American musical genius.[10]

In her presentation of the chronology of the development of these two musical genres, Burnim discusses an emerging "perceptual rift between the folk and the educated elite." This parallels a similar observation noted in results from the national survey: that although music was an important element of most worship services, "churches which have pastors with a seminary degree or higher are less likely to use spirituals in their services than those with no formal training or some Bible college or some ministry training."[11] We believe that seminaries and other educational institutions offer the history and the story behind the evolution of the musical genres. Much is owed to Burnim and others whose painstaking research has greatly contributed to our knowledge and the literature in the field. The challenge as we see it is for pastoral leaders, especially the seminary educated, to accept the responsibility to inform their congregations that the spirituals tell the story of the African American struggles, pains, and triumphs. They are moving testimony of "how we got over." It is a tale that we must tell.

When the use of other forms of music was surveyed, relatively few pastors reported the use of modern gospel music (29 percent). Some congregations use dance or drama in very limited ways as part of their worship services. Very few include gospel rap as part of their services. However, diversity in music types enhances the spiritual vitality in all African American congregations.[12]

Melva Wilson Costen observes that

even with increases in diversified ministries and congregational involvement in the total life of the community, spawned by faith experiences in worship, fresh ways of praising God in Jesus the Christ will burst forth in new and old ways of singing, preaching, praying, and offering thanks. The liturgy, God's work through the people, will continue through drama, dance, and the sharing of songs across cultures.[13]

The Content and Quality of Preaching

In African American congregations preaching has always held a significant place in worship. Indeed the foundations of black preaching were laid in the context of other cultural expressions of songs, fellowship, and celebration. When the slave ancestors were converted to the Christian faith, the element of storytelling, already in the African tradition, was woven into the fabric of their fellowship experiences. An important and observable feature of black preaching is the two kinds of simultaneous interrelationships going on, the interaction between the preacher and the Spirit and the interaction between the preacher and the hearer, the pulpit and the pew. These interrelationships are demonstrated as an antiphonal attribute of "call and response" so characteristic of black worship.

Black preaching as telling the story became a natural focus within the emerging faith tradition. The black preacher is fundamentally a storyteller. Good black preaching is the skillful use of language to make the story come alive as the black preacher uses a range of figures of speech to communicate ideas, thoughts, and feelings about relationship with the Supreme Being and the God who is present with the congregation in all the experiences of daily living. The Bible is the source of those stories as the characters and themes are explored. However, wherever the preacher starts and goes with stories, there is always identification with Jesus, Calvary, and "early Sunday morning."

Preaching and Motivation to Service

Homileticians often emphasize the nexus between content and behavioral purpose. Does the focus on "God's love and care" offer merely personal assurance to the believer? Or does this knowledge motivate the hearer to express that love in relation to others? This love is expressed through service, which is defined by the command under which it is performed: "Love thy neighbor as thyself" (Luke 10:27). The question is haunting in its insistence:

> When I needed a neighbour, were you there, were you there?
> When I needed a neighbour, were you there?
> And the creed and the colour and the name won't matter,
> Were you there?[14]

In Luke 10:27, Jesus is speaking to the listener, but it is the neighbor whom he is describing. I may find it easy to love Jesus and have great difficulty in loving my neighbor — the hungry, the thirsty, the imprisoned, the sick. Yet I may not love Jesus apart from loving my neighbor. Our neighbors — others — are gifts from God and opportunities for us to express our love for God. In this situation, I meet Jesus Christ in my neighbor, but my neighbor meets Jesus Christ in me. The option for the neighbor goes to the very heart of humans' response to God. The ongoing challenge is to combine genuine spiritual experience with a real passion for improving the welfare of persons in the social-economic-political order.

The national survey sought to discover the content emphasis of sermons. The overwhelming majority of pastors feel that their sermons "always" focus on God's love and care (83 percent), personal spiritual growth (74 percent), and practical advice for daily living (66 percent). Comparatively few report that their sermons always focus on social justice (26 percent), references to racial situations in society (17 percent), or references to black liberation theology or womanist theology (12 percent). It is interesting to observe that black Presbyterians and black United Methodists are less likely than others to report that their sermons "always" focus on practical advice for daily living and personal spiritual growth. In terms of sermon focus, no statistically significant differences emerged based on size of congregations.[15]

Not by Sermon Alone

There was a tale that came to life when one of us was in seminary. It coincided with an animal disease that was creating quite a stir in those days. One of the Latin American countries bred cattle from which corned beef was made. The cattle that contracted that disease were said to have had "foot and mouth" disease. Just like the more recent "mad cow" disease, it had an adverse effect on the industry. A clever person in seminary used the malady of the cattle to suggest that we should be different from many ministers who, as he described them, were suffering from "foot and mouth" disease — they didn't visit and couldn't preach.

Another way of looking at the connection between visiting and preaching is to use two biblical symbols for our work. The symbol of the fish appears on many cars. Sometimes it is just a line drawing. At other times the Greek word *ichthus* appears in the body of the fish. The symbol is intended to proclaim that the drivers/owners are Christians, followers of Jesus Christ, and perhaps more specifically the implication is that they are fishers of others (Mark 1:17). The other symbol less widespread in use is the shepherd's crook, generally used by bishops. It represents the bishop in the pastoral role. But the bishop may be understood as chief shepherd. And in an ordination charge, the preacher reminds the candidates that their work is by "hook and crook." He impresses on them the importance of 'fishing' for as well as caring, as a pastor, for the souls of those entrusted to them. Caring for persons through visiting, but more importantly through listening to them, enables the preacher to learn of their needs, their deep concerns, their anxieties, their dreams, their hopes, their joys — in short, the human condition. It equally increases the relevance of the message.

Preaching and Congregational Life

Melody McCloud is an obstetrician and gynecologist in Atlanta. She is also a person of deep faith, committed earnestly to discovering and finding the life of faith meaningful for everyday living. But she is disaffected by her experience in congregations with which she has sought affiliation. She expresses feelings about her experiences as participant-observer in a poem, which was shared with us. We believe that what she is saying in the poem, sections of which are included below, offers one window into aspects of congregational life and alerts us to some challenges demanding attention.

Among some concerns she names the following: the seeming hiatus between "church" — an expression used to describe the Sunday worship experience — and its carryover into obedient and faithful living in all of its dimensions; an undue obsession with "church" and the neglect of family life; and more importantly the limiting of the meaning of being in "church" in such a way that it results in the abandonment of outreach in service to others. Our values as Christians are to be determined by the standards of Jesus Christ, not by the marketplace. There, the scales place value on bigger and costlier goods, and the merchants engage in vigorous competition, vying to outbid and get ahead of one another. In the Christian community, we seek not to pit ourselves against one another or boast of our achievements and be seduced by what some call "the edifice complex" — "my (church) house is bigger than yours." Rather we seek to live our lives in faithfulness and in obedient service that glorifies God. Melody's observations may be described as caricatures or invitations to critical self-analysis of congregational life.

TODAY'S BLACK CHURCH: GOD'S HOUSE?

How sacred Your House used to be,
with Word and prayer and hymns.
Your spirit, miracles did abide,
and cleansing from one's sins.

It no longer is about Your Word
Or living a life that's true;
From the pulpit to the door
"Church" has forsaken You.

A better "step," the longest "shout,"
"Most members on the roll";
The loudest "hoop," or flashiest robe
For sure is now the goal.

When folk depart from what's called "church"
There's one thing on their mind:
Not the lessons in Your Word,
But "Child, we had a time!"

If you ask, as they depart,
What the sermon was about...
They're not too sure, but they know
Who sure did dance and shout.

A one-hour concert each Sunday morn
Is not what my soul needs;
I want the Word "broken down"
On which I grow and feed.

No time for family, nor the sick;
For sure, none for the poor.
So busy shoutin' and meetin' and carryin' on
Behind the church house doors.

The same ol' meetings every week;
What exactly is the point?
Same stuff, different day;
Yet they trust You do anoint.

If all that works for you, fine.
Go, and do rejoice.
My spirit's in a different place;
Praise God I have a choice.

Don't need a church considered "high,"
Nor dance or lengthy "jams';'
Give me song, prayer and the Word.
Just speak, oh great I AM.

Lord, guide me to a holy place
More sacrosanct and true;
Until then, on Sunday morns,
I'm home just me and You.[16]

Congregational life is about balance and the integration of worship, work, and witness. An appeal often heard in sermons is "Can I get a witness?" It is sometimes interpreted as an invitation to affirm what the preacher is saying. The preacher is not a performer, but essentially a witness — one telling the story and pointing to Jesus and the cross. Any affirmation about what is being proclaimed should also mean that the hearer is moved to act in a way that responds to the appeal in the sermon. So if the statement highlights areas of weakness in our own spiritual life — the harboring of resentment against a fellow member for whatever reason — then we must determine and make the choice for change of behavior. Or if the Word moves us to feelings of pity for the poor and homeless, we need to find ways of response, individually and in community, giving the kind of compassion that makes a difference. Compassion is not a mere feeling of pity, but a willingness to be available

FIGURE 1.1. ASSIMILATION OF NEW PERSONS

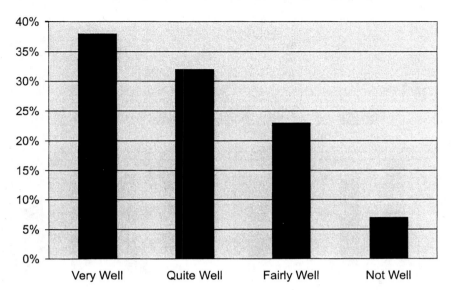

The strong majority of churches in the total sample of black churches do well in assimilating new persons into their life and fellowship.

to God on behalf of others. It is working to transform worship in the sanctuary into work in the world that makes credible witness to God in our lives.

Assimilating New Members

The strong majority of churches in the total sample of black congregations do well in assimilating new persons into their life and fellowship (see figure 1.1). One reading of the statistics might suggest that this is an important action item for many churches. When this concern is placed alongside other aspects of the survey, it is to be noted that diversity of programs, the worship experience, and denominational identity are contributing factors to the retention of new members. In the national profile, "Historically black churches report more acceptance than other Christian groups (72 percent). And acceptance of new members is rated even more highly among some World religions (Baha'is, Mormon, and Muslim) (80 percent), which include faith groups that are growing at an exceptionally rapid rate."[17]

FIGURE 1.2. ASSIMILATION IN BAPTIST CHURCHES

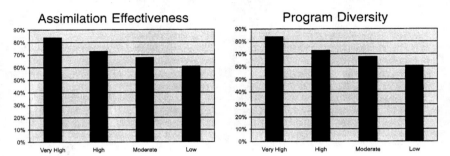

The effectiveness with which Baptist congregations assimilate new persons and retain them as members is not related to region of the country or rural-urban location (see figure 1.2). These characteristics are also reflected among some of the other historically black denominations studied. Larger churches have the advantage of offering program diversity and worship experience. However, size is not that important; larger churches are only slightly more likely than smaller churches to incorporate new persons easily.

The congregation is a place to belong in relationship, not only with one another but also most importantly with God. We may express it as an intertwining relationship with God, self, and others. Personal piety is expressed in vertical as well as horizontal relationships — upward to God and inevitably outward to others.

Congregations welcome new people all the time. These persons are retained, however, as they are nurtured, assisted to learn the congregation's story, become aware of its ethos, and are given opportunities to share their gifts and thus become involved fully in the life of that congregation. Where persons do not have these experiences and are not made to feel welcomed, they cycle out as readily as they cycle in to the life of that congregation. Congregational life should provide many opportunities for persons to grow in the faith. They should assist persons in their search and exploration into an integrated experience where faith coincides with values.

How Kathy Got Involved

The issue of assimilation arises at the point when new members are brought into the fellowship. It is also an issue of creating and making opportunities for all persons to experience a sense of belonging and participation in the life of the community. And some persons are waiting to be asked to share in the congregation's work. This was Kathy's tale. She had been divorced for three years. She had no children and returned to live in the security of her parents' home. When asked to share in one of the ministries of her congregation, she readily responded. As she expressed it, that invitation to service would fill a void in her life, would give it new meaning and purpose. Kathy continued to give and assume leadership responsibilities to the enrichment of her own life and the furthering of the ministry of that congregation.

The New Testament offers adoption as one of the ways of entry into the household of faith. In Romans 8:12–17, Paul explores ways in which we enter the family of God. There is nothing we can do to earn that place, nor deserve it. God, the loving Parent through amazing grace, has taken the lost, debt-laden sinner, hopeless and helpless, and adopted that one into the family. George Thompson uses the concept and process of adoption to suggest ways a new pastor can find welcome and a place in a new congregation.[18] It can be similarly argued that we need to explore creative ways in which new persons become members, how they are introduced into the family of a local church and participate in the flow of its life. We need to identify and break down those barriers, whatever they are, that prevent full participation in the life of that community of faith.

Strategies for Assimilation

Persons are looking for a place to belong and experience a sense of community. They are searching for meaning in life and meaningful relationships. They are also looking for an opportunity to share and use their perceived gifts and talents in satisfying and worthy engagement. As they turn to the congregation as a source of satisfaction for these longings in their souls, we need to ensure they are lovingly received, related to God, nurtured, and prepared to engage in labor that brings the realm of God nearer in everyday life.

Life in a congregation is a community adventure. We do not walk alone. Human life needs company. We have companions — the word comes from *cum panis* (with bread). We are to share bread with those who walk with us, along life's way, so that no one goes hungry. On the journey we look out for one another, ensuring that the needs and the comforts of others are met:

> Community is the spirit, the guiding light of the tribe, whereby people come together in order to fulfill a specific purpose, to help others fulfill their purpose, and to take care of one another. The goal of community is to make sure that each member of the community is heard and is properly giving the gifts they have brought to this world. Without this giving, the community dies. And without community, the individual is left without a place where they can contribute. And so the community is the grounding place where people come and share their gifts and receive them from others.[19]

Small groups are means for affirming, developing, and strengthening community. But they are equally opportunities for enabling persons to become part of and find a place in community where their gifts are shared and they can make a contribution to community life. This was what Willie Lee found when his wife, Martha Mae, was dying of cancer, yet he was faithful in coming to Bible study on Wednesday nights. The group would spend an hour or so sharing answers to the questions they had worked on during the week since last they met. As they listened to the stories from others, they found similarities with their own. Then little stories emerged of how the Word was coming alive in their lives. On one such occasion, Willie Lee sought permission from his group to share what was on his mind, and very much on his heart — his wife's dying. Members listened with great respect and deep compassion to how he had to minister to her every need — in the little things as well as the more difficult chores. This prompted others to share, and then prayer followed for Willie Lee and Martha Mae and for themselves, grateful that they could share one another's burdens. Martha Mae, Willie Lee's wife, died a few months after those moments shared in Bible study. Their lives touched one another's. They knew then what it was to belong to a community of faith in which members support and draw strength from one another for their common journey.

At the dawn of this new millennium our lives in society are increasingly characterized by bureaucratic control and depersonalizing technologies. Many persons are turning for deliverance to small groups where they experience deep interpersonal relationships with others who share their fundamental beliefs and values. Vital congregations provide many such possibilities for enhancing and enriching our common life.

Checklist for Chapter 1

- Discover and list those things that reflect the culture of your congregation.
- Observe and note the different styles of music and worship offered in your congregation.

- Plan to listen to sermons that you hear in your congregation in one month and note the themes of each sermon.

- List the number of ways that your congregation seeks to include new persons into your fellowship.

Questions for Discussion, Reflection, and Action

1. Are new persons welcomed because your congregation is open and friendly?

2. Is there love for one another, working together, and commonality in your community of faith, or is there discord?

3. Is there openness to different ideas and expressions in your congregation, or are members expected to think alike, have shared goals and values, speak the same language, and hold the party line?

4. Recall a recent sermon and reflect on how its message moved you to change your behavior or your lifestyle. What were the main ideas in the sermon?

5. Are there care groups in your congregation where persons develop supportive, open, healing, and trusting relationships with others in which all experience and express the love of God in Jesus Christ?

~ *Two* ~

CONGREGATIONAL PROFILES

If the whole body were an eye, where would the hearing be?
If the whole were hearing, where would the sense of smell
be? But as it is, God arranged members in the body, each as
he chose. — 1 Corinthians 12:17–19

The business of the church cannot always be separated from
the business of society for a man or a woman is both soul and
body, and to salvage one often requires healing the other.
— Gardner C. Taylor

In this chapter you will learn about

- exploring and examining differences in your own congregations as compared to the national profile
- characteristics of black churches related to congregational size, space, and facilities
- how to develop an assessment of your own congregation

In the Corinthian church of the first century, Paul had to answer questions relating to how the people of this congregation should test for the usefulness of gifts of the Spirit. Just how was one to measure who had what gifts? How were they to know if these gifts were truly from the Holy Spirit? How could they "test" for these gifts? What criteria were to be used? These were pressing questions in early Christianity.

Paul states that there is only one positive criterion for testing those who claim to have the gifts of the Holy Spirit: the Holy Spirit through Jesus Christ inspires all gifts. But while there is only one criterion, there are many spiritual gifts. And the variety of gifts is inspired by one and same Spirit. The diversity of gifts is given to everyone for the common good. Paul uses the analogy of the body to emphasize the image of one organism with its many different members. Since Paul understands the church to be "the body of Christ," he can speak of Christ as a corporate figure with many diverse members. Paul teaches that the individual members of the community have their own proper function and that these functions are not the same or interchangeable. If it is true that not all members of the human body can be eyes or ears, then it is also true that the Christian community needs many diverse gifts but still remains one and the same body. Paul also adds that just as the different members of the body are interdependent and need each other, so also do Christians. There are not only different gifts but also different functions and ministries that must be used for the common good.

As congregations participate in the ongoing process of studying their life, clarifying the context of their particular characteristics can give meaning to their experience. This chapter will offer ways to explore and examine differences between the national profile of black Protestant churches and your own congregation, and will help in the development of a congregational assessment.

Location

Each congregation is within itself a community and operates within its larger denominational entity, within the community of black Christian Protestant denominations, and within American Protestant denominations as a whole. In a comparative study of your congregation with both other black Protestant denominations and other U.S. denominations, an important point to examine is location.

There are over 405,000 Christian places of worship in the United States, including 100,000 with no affiliation to any other group.[1] Of all Christian traditions, Protestants have produced the greatest variety of denominations and churches although there is no accurate count of the total number of congregations in the U.S. Protestant churches combined account for over half of the U.S. population with the number of Christians who attend church higher in the United States than any Western country. The largest Protestant denominational headquarters are in the eastern half of the United States. As for the fastest-growing congregations, most are located in the eastern half of the United States also, although California has the greatest number of huge churches. It is estimated that over 100,000 independent charismatic congregations have sprung up across the United States since 1980 (see figure 2.1).

FIGURE 2-1. DISTRIBUTION OF BLACK CHURCHES BY REGION IN THE UNITED STATES

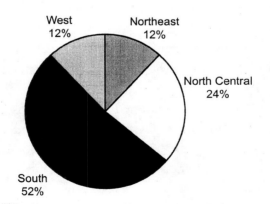

Over half of the black churches in the total sample of black Protestant congregations are located in the South.

Does geography have anything to do with congregational life? Yes, geography matters. It helps a congregation know and understand the context for ministry God is calling them to do. The black church's foundational value is holism. This means that the ministry and mission of the black church address the needs of the whole individual and the whole community. From the early days of the church a holistic ministry was taken for granted: religion always included survival as well as spiritual needs. The church's concern for the whole person is anchored in the teachings and ministry of Jesus Christ.

Congregations today are being asked to view themselves differently than they have for hundreds of years. They are now being asked to link the global and the local. Americans are bombarded with contradictory information that summons a world of polar extremes. Constant references in the media to the significance of global factors serve as reminders of the impotence of individual efforts. Just when we think that any individual action is futile, the Million Man March, followed two years later by the Million Woman March, hammers home the message that individuals need to take greater responsibility for the shaping of their lives and the lives of those around them. President Clinton and Colin Powell gave official sanction to the need for greater individual investment in local communities when they unveiled the President's Volunteer Summit in Philadelphia in the spring of 1997.

Few congregations are equipped to view themselves in these broad and challenging ways. First let us understand where we are historically within the black Protestant church. Second, let us understand how religion is categorized in America. Third, let us view the geographical growth patterns of black congregations. These three perspectives will give historical understanding of major black Protestant groups in the United States and give definition of religious groups as they are viewed in the United States.

A Historical Perspective

About 87 percent of black Christians in the United States were either Baptist or Methodist in 1965, with Baptists comprising 65 percent of that number. Recent growth in Pentecostal denominations, especially the Church of God in Christ (COGIC), has reduced the Baptist proportion, but it is still more than half. Baptist membership is grouped into a large number of denominations, some very large and many quite small. The COGIC denomination is the largest Pentecostal denomination in the world today. Its large increase in membership since 1965 is attributed to the rapid growth of evangelical Protestant churches throughout the United States. In fact,

FIGURE 2.2. DISTRIBUTION OF HISTORICALLY BLACK DENOMINATIONS IN THE SOUTH

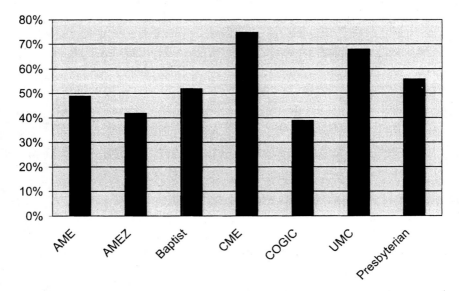

This chart shows the high percentage of black churches in the total sample that are located in the South. UMC and Presbyterian percentages reflect only black members within these denominations.

in both white and black denominations, the phenomenal growth in evangelical Protestant churches since 1945 has put new face on American religion.

Beginning as a lay movement within the Church of England, Methodism expanded over the years between 1738 and 1790 under the leadership of John Wesley and Charles Wesley. By 1775 the true center of Methodism in the United States lay in the South. Toward the end of the eighteenth century large groups of African Americans seceded from old-line Methodism and formed independent churches: the African Methodist Episcopal Church (AME), 1787; the African Methodist Episcopal Zion Church (AMEZ), 1796; and in 1844 the most devastating split of all, the bisecting of the Methodist Episcopal Church into northern and southern bodies. The cause of this major split was, of course, slavery. In an amicable agreement between white and black members of the Methodist Episcopal Church in the South, in 1870 the Colored Methodist Episcopal Church (CME) was formed. In 1954 the name was changed to the Christian Methodist Episcopal Church (CME). This is the largest African American Methodist denomination. Although numerically the Christian Methodist Episcopal Church still holds the largest numbers of black members in the Methodist denomination, the COGIC denomination, as part of the evangelical Protestant movement, has experienced the fastest growth since 1995.[2]

Protestant Denominational Categories

Although the majority of newer black congregations are to be found in the western part of the United States, this is not true for all major black denominations. The AME and CME denominations have exhibited their greatest growth in the West, but in comparison to other black denominations, this growth was less than 10 percent. The greatest growth for the CME denomination was in the north central portion of the United States. Regionally this area is defined

**FIGURE 2.3. GROWTH BY CATEGORIZATION
OF U.S. DENOMINATIONS, 1990-k–2000**

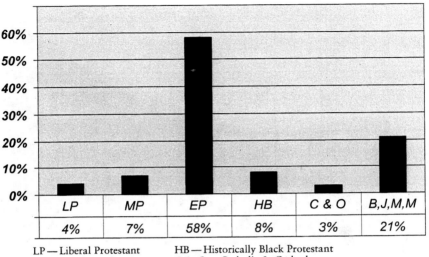

	LP	MP	EP	HB	C & O	B,J,M,M
	4%	7%	58%	8%	3%	21%

LP — Liberal Protestant   HB — Historically Black Protestant
MP — Moderate Protestant   C & O — Catholic & Orthodox
EP — Evangelical Protestant   B, J, M, M — Baha'is, Jewish, Mormon, Muslim

as the industrial Midwest and consists of eight states: Illinois, Indiana, Michigan, Missouri, Ohio, Pennsylvania, West Virginia, and Wisconsin. Figure 2.3 reflects a growth trend in American religion during the period 1990–2000. It highlights the significant upsurge in Evangelical Protestantism. Black churches, like liberal and moderate Protestant churches, exhibited minimal growth during this period.

Location of Black Congregations by Region

The AMEZ denomination since 1965 has experienced phenomenal growth in the West, mainly in Arizona, Nevada, and California. This accounts for 75 percent of the denomination's growth in this region of the country. The westward expansion in numbers also includes the Baptist denomination. However, proportionally

FIGURE 2.4. CHURCHES BEGUN AFTER 1965

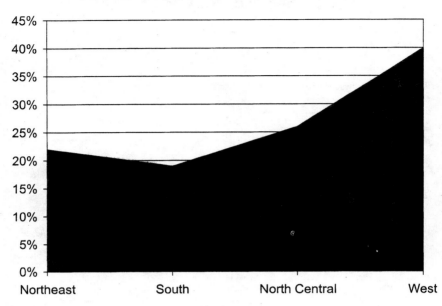

Black churches organized after 1965 are more likely in the western part of the United States.

more Baptist congregations were organized between 1966 and 2000 in the Northeast than in the total sample of black churches. COGIC churches, as the fastest growing black denomination, have experienced high growth numbers across the country. Presbyterian churches have followed the national averages, and the majority of their churches in the West have experienced growth. Black churches in the United Methodist denomination experienced 50 percent of its growth in western churches, and the churches in Texas also have experienced explosive growth. Figure 2.4 illustrates the exponential growth of black churches in the west after 1965. Figure 2.5 is a breakdown by percentage of historically black Protestant denominations by region. This corresponds to data shown in figure 2.4.

**FIGURE 2.5. CHURCHES ORGANIZED BY DENOMINATION
IN DIFFERENT REGIONS AFTER 1965**

	Northeast	*South*	*North Central*	*West*
AME	0%	3%	2%	8%
AMEZ	8%	2%	18%	75%
Baptist	35%	21%	24%	39%
CME	8%	7%	17%	7%
COGIC	52%	49%	45%	53%
Presbyterian	0%	9%	6%	29%
UMC	0%	10%	17%	50%

In discussion of regional growth after 1965, figure 2.5 illustrates that different black denominations have experienced various levels of growth after 1965. For example, the COGIC denomination has experienced 49 percent growth in the South. The CME denomination shows for that region only 7 percent growth in the same period.

Getting in Touch with the Congregation's Background

Your congregation is a human institution located in history (the date it was founded to the present), in a specific place in geography (your community), and in the lives of its members. These three aspects of your congregation will help you analyze and understand the circumstances in which your congregation operates. For this reason we suggest you study your congregation using a format developed by Nancy L. Eiesland and R. Stephen Warner that will help you to see your congregation in context within its community.[3] This method for exploring a congregation allows the congregation to be viewed as a unit interacting with other units of society: people, organizations, and culture.

Through participation in specific exercises, groups within a congregation can divide the work into manageable pieces. One group looks at the congregation historically; another group looks at the congregation as part of a community; and a third explores how members interact with the congregation in relation to the rest of their lives. By establishing such a process, you will identify and better meet the challenges of both the present generation of members and upcoming generations.

Congregational Time Line

One good way to understand how the congregation is situated in its local, denominational, and national history is to create a congregational time line. This exercise is relatively simple and can be completed in a short period of time — an evening or maybe over a series of "Wednesday night suppers." Creating a congregational time line involves a mix of memories that will help newer and long-time members see how the congregation operated in larger societal events. It will help discover links between external demographics, cultural and organizational shifts, and the internal stresses and strains historically experienced by the congregation. It may even uncover the reason for certain behaviors of your congregation. Here is a humorous example one young pastor experienced in trying to understand the meaning behind an internal strain he found in his congregation:

> A young pastor found a serious problem in his new congregation. During the Sunday service, half the congregation stood for the prayers and half remained seated, and each side shouted at the other, insisting that theirs was the true tradition. Nothing the pastor said or did moved toward solving the impasse. Finally, in desperation, the young pastor sought out the church's 99-year-old founder. He met the old pastor in the nursing home and poured out his troubles. "So tell me," he pleaded, "was it the tradition for the congregation to stand during the prayers?"

"No," answered the old pastor.

"Ah," responded the younger man, "then it was the tradition to sit during the prayers?"

"No," answered the old pastor.

"Well," the young pastor responded, "what we have is complete chaos! Half the people stand and shout, and the other half sit and scream."

"Ah," said the old man, "that was the tradition."

The time line is exactly what it says it is — a historical depiction of the life of a congregation as remembered by its members. It becomes a story about the congregation.

Storytelling is a treasured art within African American culture. In the early church in American history, black Christians had little concern for adherence to denominational polity, recitation of creeds, or following of predetermined liturgical action. From the African taproot, the early shapers of black folk religion forged a Christian worldview, or "sacred cosmos," that permeates all of life.[4] Melva Wilson Costen, a leading scholar on African American worship experiences, found the methodology used to develop a black theology was honed from "folk methods" common to Africans and transported wherever Africans are in the Diaspora. Music, song, and storytelling by the *griot* (a West African term for "one who is gifted in the art of communicating wisdom, ideas, historical events, morals, etc.") became the major means of shaping, documenting, and distributing folk theology.[5]

A congregational time line can be shaped to suit the particular focus of your congregational study. A method often used in creating time lines is to record both a vertical and horizontal line. The horizontal line would be organized chronologically beginning when your congregation first was established. The vertical line would report specific events related to your church and could also record community, regional/state, national, and world events that occurred at the same time. This exercise is especially helpful to younger congregants who often do not have historical contexts for events in history and the ways events connect. Encourage members of your congregation to reflect on significant moments, especially local happenings as well as larger patterns or events.

The time line exercise is an excellent way to develop an informal history. More importantly, this exercise will allow congregational members to tell their stories and become involved in the congregational study process. Remember, the goal of a congregational time line is to uncover the communal memory of the congregation on the basis of personal and group remembrance.

Investigating the Community for Your Congregation

There are practical pressures facing many churches today: political, societal, economic, and familiar, to name a few. Additionally, we are living at a time of rapid change. The Internet and television are changing the landscape of our lives. Society is becoming increasingly complex. Churches are increasingly expected to help solve many of society's ills that they did not create. What is a church to do? Whatever we do as church people we need to underscore that the work must be done with God's direction. As Christians we have Jesus Christ as the model for our lives. Jesus always was looking for where God was at work and joined God in that work. Jesus did not have to guess what to do. Jesus did not have to dream up what he could do for God. He watched to see what God was doing around his life, and Jesus put his life there.

As members participate in a study of their congregation, they try to understand God's calling for their church. No one individual has the total vision for God's desire for a local church. A church needs to hear the whole counsel of God through the Bible, prayer, and circumstances. A church comes to know what God wants it to do when the whole body understands what Christ — the head — is saying to them. "Now I appeal to you, brothers and sisters, by the name of our Lord Jesus Christ, that all of you be in agreement and that there be no divisions among you, but that you be united in the same mind and the same purpose" (1 Cor. 1:10).

The following section is concerned with discovering the relationship of the congregation to its community. The congregational time line allowed you to see who you were in relation to your congregational members. This next exercise will allow you to see your church in relation to your local community. It is an important step in preparing to hear God's call to your church. The exercise will allow you to understand where your congregation is socially, physically, and economically. The purposes of the exercise will help you

- discover things in the neighborhood that are new;

- recognize things that are so familiar that they are not noticed;

- think about your congregation in relation to its community; and

- help with an understanding of increasingly complex interests and needs of congregants.

"Tools" your congregation will use include

- using teams of congregants with different age representatives in order to get a wide range of perspectives, and

- recording the perspectives to develop reports and understanding among congregants.

Activities for this phase of congregational assessment include

- *Looking.* Depending upon where your congregation is located (rural, urban, or suburban location), taking a walk or driving around your church community will help you discover things in the neighborhood. A second purpose is to recognize things that may have become so familiar that they are not noticed, for example, who is on the sidewalk at various times of the day and night; who gets on and off the bus at what time; what intersections are particularly busy and at what times; what properties have become such eyesores that they escape attention; and where exactly the firehouse and the police station are located.

- *Asking questions.* At the end of each chapter of this book there are suggested questions recommended to engage your congregation in discovering your identity as a community of faith. These questions are offered to begin the reflection process.

- *Reading.* Read local news articles, your congregational time line, and other documents your church has created over the years to see what groundwork was laid for particular ministries and what ministries your congregation has successfully or unsuccessfully undertaken.

Exploring Members' Networks

The third activity to understand the context of your congregants' lives is to explore members' network maps. This information will help you to see how the congregation fits into patterns of meaning for its members. These maps are largely formed by the routines of work, leisure, and how congregants "move" through your community. The maps will not only tell you how congregants get from one place to another; they reveal pictures of community relations and organizational ties. They may also uncover how different constituencies within your congregation relate to your geographical location. It is best to have just a few persons in your congregation complete this task, depending on the size of your congregation. The purpose is to have representatives of each constituency in your congregation complete a map, for example, long-time resident, newcomer, member of an ethnic group. The persons completing the maps should be volunteers.

In their essay "Ecology: Seeing the Congregation in Context," Nancy Eiesland and R. Stephen Warner offer this exercise to help complete an understanding of meaningful patterns and networks your congregational members have developed.[6] For this exercise you will need detailed maps of your community, pushpins, and colored yarn. Begin by dividing participants into groups representing significant constituencies within the congregation. Have a volunteer within each constituency place a pushpin at their home location with several long pieces of yarn attached. The volunteers then place pins at other significant points on the map indicating where the church is, their places of work, primary shopping venues, schools of their children and so on. Extend the yarn from the home location to the other points on the map. Other participants within the constituency participating in this exercise can discuss differences and similarities in their networks. When patterns are revealed and compared to the patterns of other constituencies within the congregation, it becomes possible to see ways involvement in the congregation have emerged. These perspectives are often exciting points to begin further discussions about the congregation. The three exercises described above are tools that will enable you to better consider how your congregation is connected to its community. The following charts offer additional resources for understanding the people, cultural meanings, and relations that make up the social fabric of your congregation.

Rural-Urban-Suburban Locations

Rural, urban, and suburban locations each offer specific challenges. Urban neighborhoods are often economically depressed. They are often ridden with a high crime rates, high teenage pregnancy rates, under- and unemployment, inadequate housing, poor schools, low business investment, and weak political participation.

Rural areas are even more sensitive to these issues. Poor schools, under- and unemployment, low wages, teenage pregnancy, and low

**FIGURE 2.6. DISTRIBUTION OF CHURCHES
IN RURAL-URBAN LOCATIONS**

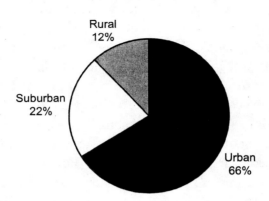

Most of the black churches are located in urban areas.

business investment are often accompanied by traditional mores of self-sufficiency and quiet forbearance. It is interesting to note, however, that small businesses often play a major and vital role in the economic activities of urban and rural communities.[7]

Suburban churches have their challenges also. Although they do not experience the severe economic problems of urban and rural churches, they do face questions related to social distancing. Concerning this problem, C. Eric Lincoln and Lawrence H. Mamiya, in their study of black Christianity based on interviews with more than eight hundred African American clergy, conclude:

> The membership of the seven historic black denominations is composed largely of middle-income working-class and middle-class members. But Black pastors and churches have had a difficult time in attempting to reach the hard-core urban poor, the black underclass, which is continuing to grow.... The challenge for the future is whether black clergy and their churches will attempt to transcend class boundaries and reach out to the

poor, as these class lines continue to solidify with demographic changes in black communities.[8]

Congregational Size

Over half of the churches in the total sample of black churches have fewer than one hundred regularly participating adult members (28 percent have under fifty members). Because of the way churches are organized in the United States, many churches have small congregations, whether they are urban or rural. This is problematic because congregations cannot raise the money to pay for a minister themselves and have to subsidize pastor's salaries denominationally. These small churches are an American phenomenon, and churches rarely are prepared to contemplate amalgamation as a solution to the "problem" of the small, subsidized church.

Recently, several studies on small churches found that one of the keys to helping them become financially viable is to rebuild the confidence of the congregation. What does building the confidence of the congregation mean?

FIGURE 2.7. BLACK CHURCHES WITH UNDER ONE HUNDRED REGULARLY PARTICIPATING ADULT MEMBERS

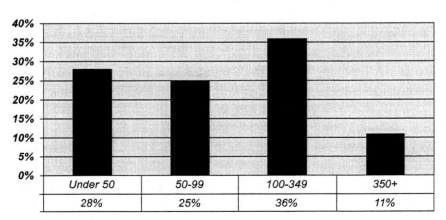

Under 50	50-99	100-349	350+
28%	25%	36%	11%

FIGURE 2.8. DISTRIBUTION OF CHURCHES IN RURAL-SUBURBAN-URBAN LOCATIONS.

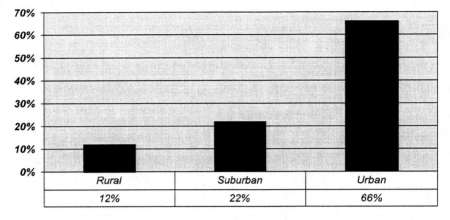

Rural	Suburban	Urban
12%	22%	66%

Most black churches are located in urban areas. Figure 2.8 reflects the distribution.

In the Epistles we find the future of the new Christian church depended on an "all-member ministry." Each member who joined the emerging Christian churches expected to participate in the ongoing ministries of the church. It was out of this all-member church ministry that Paul wrote about the importance of each member to the congregation (see 1 Cor. 12:12–31; Eph. 4:14–16). Confidence comes from understanding that each congregation is part of Christ's body and needs the gifts of each member, even those who feel unimportant. When each member is cared for and emphasized, dissension is prevented and confidence is built. When a congregation is growing in confidence, the ministry and mission can continue and develop even if unexpected or catastrophic events occur in the life of the congregation. A congregation builds its confidence by including all members so that the gifts experienced within the congregation can be released and used in ministry within the church and its mission in the community where it is located. It's about ordained and lay Christians sharing responsibility together for building faith and confidence that will enable the congregation to be a truly dynamic presence in our communities.

Small churches are often challenged to be congregations that are building confidence. Limited resources and limited numbers of persons within the small congregation can contribute to lack of confidence. Although this book is not a study of small congregations, those reading it may find additional resources specific to small congregations in the resources listed at the end of this chapter. A finding that earlier studies of small congregations suggested, and that was confirmed in the Project 2000 study, was that small churches can and do make a significant contribution to the present life and future work of local churches. Carl S. Dudley in his book *Making the Small Church Effective* found that the small church exemplifies traditional Christian values that often become lost in large congregations. Dudley wrote:

> In a big world, the small church has remained intimate. In a fast world, the small church has been steady. In an expensive world, the small church has remained plain. In a complex world, the small church has remained simple. In a rational world, the small church has kept feeling. In a mobile world, the small church has been an anchor. In an anonymous world, the small church calls us by name.[9]

Historical Time

Over half of the churches in the total sample of black churches Project 2000 surveyed were organized before 1945. It is noteworthy that few churches have been organized within the last decade and that growth in black churches has significantly been reduced.

The black church has contributed to the intellectual and sociopolitical culture of African American life in America. This statement

FIGURE 2.9. YEAR CONGREGATION ORGANIZED

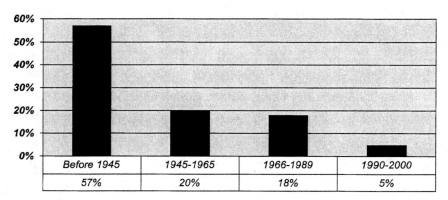

Before 1945	1945-1965	1966-1989	1990-2000
57%	20%	18%	5%

is not a surprise to anyone. What is surprising is how little is understood about how black congregations conducted their activities and played such a significant role in this intellectual and sociopolitical environment. Because African American cultural expression often follows a traditional oral expression, frequently it is not conducted formally within congregations. Black Christianity has been a source, the primary consistent source, for African American culture. Black Christianity has contributed several indispensable elements to the black struggle. First, as an indigenous institution, it supplied an organizational framework that assisted the masses to consolidate their finances, integrate ideas, and unify behind their leaders. Second, the black church gave the civil rights movement strategic and philosophical direction through leadership and support. How individual congregations accomplished their activities is important to understanding of individual congregations, to larger denominational stories, and to the even larger story within American culture. So this book is advocating that to get these important and significant stories told, the story needs to begin within the congregation.

The date of origin of a congregation contributes to its understanding of itself, how it sees its role within its immediate community, and the role it chooses to have in current societal issues. While the pastor of a church often is seen as "the public face" or "public voice," in actuality, it is the members' perceptions of themselves that define the congregation.

The role or identity of a particular congregation can be as unified, transitory, or varied as the number of congregation members that attend the church. When a congregation was created situates it at a point in history. Most black churches were established before 1945. This statement has two points of meaning. First, the period of time "before 1945" covers approximately two hundred years. Second, 1945 represents a specific marker in American history. It is the year World War II ended.

The war had created opportunities for blacks that fueled changes in the existing social order. The black church for over two hundred years had been the place of refuge for survival in America. The period immediately following the end of the war was the beginning years of the civil rights struggle. By the late 1950s activism of black rural and urban churches provided the base for the protest movement that began in 1955. Church involvement in the non-violent confrontational demand for inclusion into the American mainstream contributed to the more than 20 percent growth of black denominational churches following World War II. For eleven years beginning in 1955, as African Americans protested subordination through boycotts, sit-ins, and other nonviolent strategies, the church assumed the vanguard in the fight for liberation.[10]

The black church, on becoming the church of protest, contributed two essential elements to the African American struggle. First, it supplied an organizational framework for the emerging protest movement. Second, the church gave the movement strategic and philosophical direction through the teachings of Martin Luther King. According to King, the black masses were morally obligated to disobey unjust laws through nonviolent resistance. Thus the church contributed organizational structure and philosophical leadership to the struggle for civil rights. From the mid-1960s until the late 1980s, the church remained a stable influence. But by the late 1980s, civil rights church leaders were aging and dying. Additionally, children who had grown up in black households that benefited from the civil rights legislation created during the late 1960s and 1970s were a part of the nation's socioeconomic mainstream. This factor created two crises that threaten the viability of the black church as an institution and the stability of the community in which it operates: a class crisis and an urban crisis.

As well-prepared blacks entered the ranks of the upwardly mobile middle class, they left urban areas to live in surrounding residential neighborhoods. The inner city was abandoned to its African American underclass. At the same time, the poorly educated, unskilled urban masses were left trapped in jobless inner cities. This social distancing within the black community challenges the basic functionality of the black church.[11]

As congregations begin to examine their identity as communities of faith, some understanding of an interpretation behind the data reflected in the charts in the following sections will enable congregations to improve their capacity for meaningful ministry.

Characteristics of Growing Churches

In the total sample of black congregations studied, we found the larger the membership, the more likely a 5 percent or more growth occurred in the last five years. Reasons for this include:

- Large churches are typically situated in growing population areas.

- Larger churches are better able to have staff and volunteers.

- Larger churches have a diversity of programs that engage present members and attract new members.

Building and Growing

At the beginning of the twentieth century, W. E. B. Du Bois wrote, "The Negro church of today is the social center of Negro life in the United States, and the most characteristic expression of African character."[12] In 1909 Booker T. Washington echoed: "The Negro Church represents the masses of the Negro people. It was the first institution to develop out of the life of the Negro masses and still retains the strongest hold upon them."[13] These social conditions placed a special responsibility on black churches; they had to be social centers, political forums, schoolhouses, mutual aid societies, refuges from racism and violence, and places of worship.[14] Throughout the twentieth century as blacks moved to cities, other institutions such as fraternal groups, civil rights organizations, and social clubs developed within the black community. Although the church became less of a central institution for black culture, it continues to exert the strongest influence on black community life even today.

Religious institutions such as the church, therefore, have great importance to black life and culture. To them accrue the primary responsibility for the enhancement and development of that unique

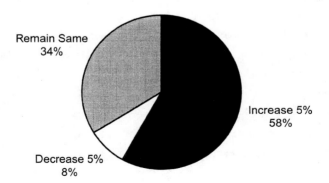

FIGURE 2.10. MEMBERSHIP GROWTH PATTERNS

Remain Same
34%

Increase 5%
58%

Decrease 5%
8%

spiritual quality that has enabled African Americans to survive and flourish under some of the most unfavorable conditions of the modern world.[15] In the past decade, the demand for churches and other faith-based organizations to solve complex social problems has escalated dramatically. The black church is increasingly expected to play a significant role in renewing American democracy.

Robert Franklin recently wrote:

> If you were to ask the average person what changes have occurred in the Black Church since the death of Martin Luther King, most would either have no idea or would think the question absurd. It's like the old joke, "How many deacons does it take to change a light bulb?" The punch line: "What do you mean, change?" Many people doubt that any changes have occurred in this most mature, bedrock institution of the Black community. But this impression belies an exciting and dynamic story that may not be apparent to the casual observer.[16]

In 2000, when we began our study of the African American religious experience as it related to social outreach programs, we decided to look at growth and diversity since 1995, and church growth in relation to the number of social outreach programs. By focusing on growth in number of program types since 1995, we felt the data would be very current and accurately reflect what is going on in black churches today. This information will help you analyze your congregation as it explores the role it plays within American society and the role it wants to play within black society.

Larger churches offer a great variety of programs to members. However, even in churches of different sizes, the greater the number of programs presented to members, the more likely the church has grown in membership since 1995. Figure 2.11 reflects the percentage of growth in churches with seven programs.

FIGURE 2.11. CONGREGATIONS HAVING 7 PROGRAMS

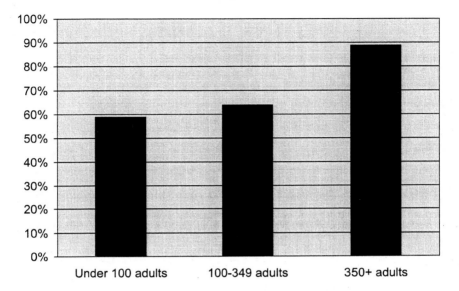

Figure 2.11 reflects how growth and number of programs are interrelated. Although the chart shows the rate of growth in congregations of varying size with seven programs (59 percent for churches with less than 100 members; 64 percent for churches with 100–349 adults; 89 percent for churches with 350+ adults), the number of programs was more significant than type of programs in our study. Even churches with five or less programs also experienced growth: 44 percent for churches with less than 100 adults; 59 percent for churches with 100–349 members; and 50 percent for churches with 350+ members.

We found that larger congregations sponsor a greater variety of social service programs for the needy in the community, but even in churches of varying size, the greater the number of social outreach programs, the more likely there was growth in membership since 1995.

FIGURE 2.12. CONGREGATIONS HAVING 0–10 PROGRAMS

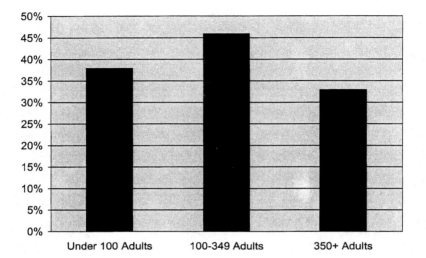

Growth and Social Outreach

Figure 2.12 reflects growth percentages in churches with less than ten social outreach programs. Larger churches that offered fourteen or fifteen social outreach programs experienced twice the growth as churches with ten or fewer programs (see figure 2.13).

With increased pressure to be involved in social outreach programs, churches face challenging questions in understanding their roles within public policy and serving those in needs. The black church has no challenger as the cultural womb of the black community. Not only did it give birth to new institutions such as schools, banks, and insurance companies, but it also provided an academy and an arena for political activities, while nurturing young talent for musical, dramatic, and artistic development. E. Franklin Frazier's apt descriptive phrase, "a nation within a nation," points to these multifarious levels of community involvement found in the black church, in addition to the traditional concerns of worship, moral nurture, education, and social development.[17]

FIGURE 2.13. CONGREGATIONS HAVING 14–15 PROGRAMS

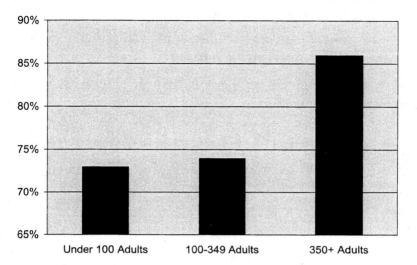

The Project 2000 study found the vast majority of black churches offer a wide diversity of social service ministries. This contributes to a strong church and spiritual vitality that will be fully discussed in chapter 5.

Checklist for Chapter 2

- Construct a congregational timeline
- Discover the community for your congregation
- Explore members' networks

Questions for Discussion, Reflection, and Action

1. In what ways can you use results from a congregational study?

2. Who will be involved in the congregational study process? What design for a congregational study do you want to have?

3. What items of information does your congregation need to gather as you plan for your ministry?

4. How do you plan to use the information you gather to address issues that the congregation is facing?

5. Is your congregation gathered around a minister or is it a ministering community?

~ Three ~

INTERNAL AND EXTERNAL MISSION-ORIENTED PROGRAMS

The Spirit of the Lord is upon me because he has anointed me to bring good news to the poor. He has sent me to proclaim release to the captives and recovery of sight to the blind to let the oppressed go free to proclaim the year of the Lord's favor.
— Luke 4:18–19

When we struggle for human rights, for freedom, for dignity, when we feel it is a ministry of the church to concern itself with those who are hungry, for those who are deprived, we are not departing from God's promise. He comes to free us from sin, and the church knows that sin's consequences are all such injustices and abuses. The church knows that it is saving the world when it undertakes to speak of such things.
— Oscar Romero

In this chapter you will learn about

- concepts and techniques for the practice of ministry

- internal and mission-oriented programming

- participation in civil rights issues

67

Jesus walks into the synagogue of Nazareth on the Sabbath day. An attendant hands him the scroll of Isaiah. Jesus unrolls it and finds the place where the lectionary for the day is the scriptural passage cited in the first epigraph above. After the reading, Jesus rolls up the scroll, gives it back to the synagogue assistant, sits down, and teaches with authority, from the chair — ex cathedra. He declares: "Today this scripture has been fulfilled in your hearing" (Luke 4:21). What a bold beginning to the ministry of Jesus. Everything that follows in the ministry of Jesus according to Luke can be seen as an enactment of God's promises of freedom made in Isaiah 61. There is no mystery to the vocation of Luke's Jesus. He is the fulfillment of God's promised liberation. The defining perspective for his ministry and ours — the essential and impelling demand — is justice for all in society, for all persons who are encompassed in the range of God's love.

Concepts and Techniques
for the Practice of Ministry

The church belongs to God's ancient purpose expressed in the call to Israel. As Israel was redeemed from slavery and became the people of God, so all who come to Christ receive mercy and become the new people of God. The church as the whole people of God is evangelistic by its very nature. Jesus, who calls us to be with him, also sends us out to join him where he is already present in a world that he died to save. The church is called to be the bearer of good news not only by *word* (in the proclamation of the gospel) but in *deed* (in a lifestyle). The rhythm of the church's life is "come" and "go." Mission is the very pulse of the church's life. We are called to go out into communities where we live and there witness to him who is Savior and Sovereign of all. The Holy Spirit leads the church to bear witness in every place.

The church is, in a profound sense, Christ visible in and for the world. The body of Christ was given for the world. In that self-giving sealed by his death and resurrection, there came into being the new community, the body of Christ, commissioned to carry out Christ's ministry in the world. Concretely, this means that each member embodies this ministry and, therefore, must constantly offer up her or his body to God in worship and service. But each member or group acts not by itself but always as part of the whole body. Cooperation between Christians and churches is not optional but demanded by the very nature and calling of the church.

The church is the instrument of God's judgment and mercy in relation to the world. The world, likewise, is the means by which the church can similarly experience the mercy and judgment of God. Indeed we are reminded that God acts in the whole of God's creation and not exclusively through the church. An illustration of this is a tale that one of our friends shared with us. In New York, as we suppose in any large city that has a subway or rail transit system, one must calculate time carefully to ensure that appointments can be kept in a timely manner. Our friend Ralph lived in the Bronx and had an important appointment in Manhattan. It was during rush hour. The stairways down to the trains are wide to accommodate crowds. One might be in a crowd and not touch another on the opposite side. That's what happened on the day of the incident. In the crowd was a paralytic on crutches. He too was attempting to catch the train, but was thrown down the stairs in the throng. Our friend said that he noticed this event, but he was nowhere near the paralytic, didn't even touch him. Ralph went on his way and caught the train. Then as it was pulling out of the station, he noticed a scruffy and dirty looking man. He could have been homeless, a wino, one from whom we might avert our gaze. But it was this man who was picking up and attending to the paralytic. The point of the illustration is to suggest that the Lord does use others who may not profess belief in Jesus Christ into discerning and doing God's will. There are many examples of this double relationship in the Scriptures. Cyrus of Persia was God's instrument of mercy to Israel (Isa. 44:28). Jonah was God's herald of mercy to Nineveh. It is by this double movement that God's purposes will finally be accomplished and the nations come to share in the glory of Zion.

Internal and Mission-Oriented Programs

As your congregation seeks to fulfill its mission, it would be useful to develop an educational program. Such a program would promote serious and regular Bible study. The learning objectives of any program would include

- providing learners with an acquaintance of the biblical text, its place and value for Christian living;

- identifying and using several resources to help learners acquire knowledge of the content of the Bible; and

- developing ways of assisting students to discover and make meaning for their individual life and for life together in the community of faith, and in the several relationships with others in the world.

The Bible is the story of the encounter between God and human beings. We often speak of the Bible as the Word of God. The Bible is not the Word of God because God speaks in words, be they Hebrew or Greek, Spanish or English. Rather God spoke in the language of a human life — that of Jesus. In him the Word became human, took flesh, and dwelt among us. Through that act of God, we know what God's will is for us human beings. We must constantly seek to match our talk about Jesus with our walk in seeking to do God's will. A popular clichéd expression in the African American experience admonishes that we must "walk the walk and talk the talk." We must constantly seek to ensure that there is a coincidence between talk and walk and walk and talk. Barry White, the gravelly voiced balladeer, has a popular song that admonishes, "Practice what you preach!"[1] The admonition raises a question that invites serious reflection: Dare you or can you practice what you preach?

Memorizing Bible verses used to be a popular and ready method of teaching the Bible. Perhaps it still occurs. Charlotte, a Chinese missionary to Cambodia, told of the amazement she experienced when one particular student returned the next week with the memory verse on the tip of his tongue. When she asked how he did it, he revealed his secret. "It was very easy," he said. "Whatever the memory verse was I tried to practice it during the week. So if the memory verse said: 'Love your neighbors,' I would try to be kind to others. So when I came back to class the next week, I would have it not only in my head, but in my heart."

Any Christian educational program will use the Bible as a source book for faith development and guidance for action and daily living. Other resources and methodologies will be used in the educational process, all of them with the overarching purpose of helping persons to deepen commitment to God and fellow human beings. There is need to increase opportunities for growing together in local congregations through Bible study, prayer, care and service groups, and common witness in communities.

Putting It Together for Action

Every good program begins with an idea — a vision of what you would like to see happen through the program conceived. For Christians and congregations, the vision is discerning what God wants you to do through your life and work to build God's reign. The vision is that clear picture of a future to which God is calling you and others. As it is articulated and shared with others, God will confirm to those who receive it what God intends for God's people.

Since the vision is a big picture, you will need to take stock of what you have of human, material, and financial resources. Finally, you must decide what you will do and commit yourself to specific, attainable, and measurable goals.

Goals are different from a vision. Goals are key steps in moving visions to reality. Goals are bound by time limitations; a vision is ongoing. A vision is always larger, greater, than what can be realized by specifically set goals. The vision generates the energy to realize the goals. Effective congregations will seek to respond to problems and the needs of people — persons with hidden hurts and hidden people with hurts. As they do their work and engage in ministry, they link the vision to the program and then link these to the source of energy and power.

After you have set some goals to develop and carry out your program, you may follow the following process cycle. The cycle is based on the premise that every congregation engaging in meaningful action for societal transformation invites its members to

- explore their identity as a community of faith;
- affirm their purpose or mission;
- develop a shared vision in response to people and their needs in communities;
- consider the possibilities of their responses, given their resources and the values they share;
- commit themselves to goals that are specific, attainable, and measurable;
- develop programmatic responses relative to those goals;
- engage in action, constantly evaluating progress toward agreed goals; and
- note the failures and mistakes, but always celebrate achievements in the power and under the guidance of God's holy spirit.

Participation in Religious Programs

There is a long history of internal nurture for survival in the black faith community, but it has never been at the exclusion of outreach ministry.

Most clergy reported that their congregations participated in a wide range of religious and social programs throughout the year. Over nine in ten congregations have Bible study, prayer, or meditation groups and community service and youth programs. Large majorities of congregants participated in the remaining activities surveyed such as spiritual retreats, parenting or marriage enrichment, theological study, and young adult or singles programs.[2]

Congregations pursue their lives in a variety of ways and generally through activities that fall in the areas of worshiping, caring, learning, and serving. Different groups, programs, or ministries enable them to invite and receive people as they are, whoever they are, and assimilate persons into their community of faith. Evangelistic efforts seek to reach out to bring other persons into their fellowship and membership. Persons find relationship with God in prayer meetings, spiritual retreats, and small faith-sharing groups, just to name a few. The Holy Spirit initiates and sustains this relationship. Educational experiences, including Bible study, membership preparation classes, doctrinal study groups, and forums on social issues, help persons not only to learn about their denominational heritage but also to be nurtured and grow in faithfulness and obedience as disciples for their Christian journey. When there are persons who are sick or in crisis, individuals and groups provide loving care for one another.

Through many service-oriented programs, members are prepared and equipped to live out their faith, responding to a world that needs to know and experience God's justice. Your congregation is called to act from the center of its own life, the culture that has been shaped through its history, and the beliefs and values that your members embrace. Your ongoing challenge is to identify the needs, evaluate your capacity for response, and act always with the awareness that God who has called you into being as people of God will equip you for the life to which you have been called.

Those Youth Programs

The research data demonstrated a high interest and investment in youth programs. It suggests that congregations may be meeting the needs of a generation of seekers. We made visits to several congregations in different cities across the nation. We asked to meet with leaders. We were excited in a number of situations to note the participation of youth in leadership responsibilities — the affirmations of the freedom they felt, the experiences they had in being heard, and the opportunities they were given in the decision-making process of their local congregations. They all attested that they were genuinely made to feel full participants in the life of their congregation. In one place, the young people spoke up and spoke out. "We are a large church, but we are working at making it feel like a family. There is a consistent statement made: 'This is our family!' There is every attempt and invitation 'to be involved,' and an assurance given that there is some place that you can minister and use your gifts."

A Model for Intergenerational Ministry

We have an ongoing concern at Interdenominational Theological Center to help students make connections between classroom learning and the practice of ministry in context. Among the initiatives that have arisen from this perspective is the Annual Parents and Youth Convocation sponsored by ITC. The faculty founder and coordinator for this event is Anne E. Streaty Wimberly, professor of Christian education. The convocation initially drew participants largely from the southeast region of the United States. However, over the last eight years, it has attracted persons from the United Kingdom and more recently from Zimbabwe, Sierra Leone, Kenya, and Cameroon. Each year the chosen theme has defined the focus for the convocation. In spring 2002 it was "Pathways to Christian Living: Making Responsible Choices in a Challenging World."

The convocation offers a model in Christian youth formation and family leadership development from a family systems orientation. It seeks to offer direction to the critical issues faced by youth and their families. More particularly, as congregations seek to confront the tension between generations, the concept and process in the convocation are a creative, imaginative, and effective way of fostering the experience of family relationship in "the village" where all can find a place to belong, find support, grow in love for one another through mutual respect, and affirm a sense of community.

As you seek to develop viable youth programs, it is essential that you recruit for service only those individuals serious about reaching youths *on youths' terms.* The nature and scope of programs you develop can be varied. They should include the imparting of biblical knowledge and spiritual formation. This foundation would help them make the right decisions as they meet challenges and make choices, particularly in the difficult teen years. A social and recreational component in any program would provide creative and constructive outlets for their energies. Finally, leadership training opportunities would help them discover and use their gifts for others.

Participation in Programs of Outreach

One Thursday night, ten members of Northminster Church assembled in the church parking lot. They were about to set out on a visit to Metro prison. The prison chaplain had called their pastor. "Could you bring some members from your church to our prison to help the residents celebrate birthdays? Bring some ice cream and cookies for about forty persons. We'll have Bible study, conversation, and fellowship."

So a group from Northminster went to Metro prison and engaged in those activities — Bible study, conversation, and more. In one of the cars (the group traveled in two cars) on the way back each person began sharing about what the event did for him or her. Allison started off. She was vice-president and trust officer for one of the commercial banks in town. It amazed her fellow passengers as she told personal details of those with whom she had spoken. She told of where they came from, whether their parents were alive, if they were married, how many children they had. Her sharing set a pattern for others in the car. They were all surprised that they had remembered so much from the conversations.

Jason summed up how they all felt: "I am so glad I went. They are all so human."

Henrietta shared with Mabel, who was closest to her, the thoughts that were in her mind: "I was scared of mixing with prisoners — those evil persons that our society had to put away. Forgive me, Lord, for forgetting that it is more blessed to give than to receive, even love."

Westwood, a much larger congregation, was in another part of town, and although Metro prison was within the natural geographic boundaries of Westwood, it had no prison ministry. Westwood had many programs and ministries, but most of them were self-directed and none was to Metro prison.

Planning and Strategizing for the Congregation's Outreach

"Conversations about social transformation really begin to be significant when the people discussing the issue speak specifically about the vision that inspires their hope; when they articulate the programmatic thrust they propose; and when they describe the source of power and sustenance available to those who commit themselves to the implementation of world changing plans."[3] Persons seek opportunities to talk about those things about which they are deeply concerned. When they get together and engage in discussion, they discover and share their feelings, beliefs, and values. They also begin to explore ways in which they can respond to and begin to effect changes in conditions about which they are disaffected.

James Baldwin, in an address to the World Council of Churches meeting in Uppsala, Sweden, in 1968, argued that a church that is unresponsive to the needs of the world around it is too expensive for the world to afford.[4] He did not mean that the church had to address all the social, political, and economic ills in the community where it was located. Rather, he was suggesting that the claim that we make that we belong to Jesus Christ lays on us the burden to be responsive to the cries and the hurts of our neighbor in God's world. We are called to act, and act beyond analysis. We are asked to take risks to act. It is possible we will make mistakes, but there is no excuse for inaction. However, it is equally important that the process of analysis include critical reflection and action. We should not settle for developing programs without reflection or engage in reflection without action. A critical question in such a process might be: Does the program you propose enhance the capacity of persons to analyze their present situation and determine and act on their own goals?

In visits to several congregations, we have invited pastors and leaders to talk about and evaluate their congregations as *learning, worshiping, caring,* and *serving* communities. This process enabled congregations not only to discover their story, but also to reflect on their life in relation to the community where they are located. One congregation on the West Coast permitted persons to express the awareness, knowledge, and involvement in their programs. The men had periodically done a free barbecue for the community. On these occasions, information was offered on job openings. A special concern was to address the needs of youth in that community. One young person in the meeting testified that he was there because the church reached out in this way and helped him to discover a new focus and meaning for his life. In winter the doors of the church opened to shelter the homeless. This congregation participated in a network of congregations that responded. As the reflection on their ministry of service continued, members recognized that there was more work to be done. They agreed that they needed to deepen their level of faith and commitment and that the life of prayer should lead them out to engagement in service to those needy persons in their community.

The community is a crucial link that connects the individual to the larger society, helping to develop a sense of belonging, shaping individual and group life. You and your congregation need to pray for eyes to *see* those who are in their midst. Can you and they acknowledge, as the poet confesses in "I Have Seen Them"?

> I have seen them trying . . .
> to sober up
> to be heard
> to listen
> to live —
>
> Lord knows, I have seen them.
> I have seen them waiting . . .
> for relief
> for a job
> for winter to pass
> for life —
>
> Yes Lord, I have seen them.
> I have seen them crying . . .
> because it's too late
> because they can't feed their babies

because they are tired of maybe
because they are afraid —

Dear Lord yes, I have seen them
praying...
for miracles.[5]

Through our ministry as Christians with persons in our world, we witness to Jesus as Savior and Sovereign with our words and our deeds. We who bear his name come under the searching light of God's judgment on all persons, and that judgment begins with us. We are called to raise some self-evaluative questions about our mission and ministry as congregations and communities of faith: whether we love persons enough to be able to witness to them or whether our witness will be false testimony; whether God can confirm our witness; whether we believe and live as if Jesus Christ died for all persons, and not only for us who profess faith in him.

Importance of Understanding and Engaging the Context

Congregations like other community sites — schools, libraries, museums, banks, police precincts, and shopping malls — are places where persons interact, work, and serve one another. In a majority of communities, people represent different ethnicities, cultures, and religions. Where congregations are unwilling to affirm these realities, they narrowly accept themselves as inwardly looking clubs, unresponsive to the needs of others. Congregations, however, need to recognize these realities in the lives of persons in a common space. Such congregations have the potential for engaging in meaningful ministry and making a difference in the lives of persons whom they meet and where they touch them.

A study of social context can document and clarify community needs and suggest strategic options for response. As you and your congregation plan for mission and ministry to context we offer the following steps for your consideration:

- Identify the boundaries of the community for which your community accepts responsibility.
- Study your local community to discover human problems and needs.
- Begin to develop a list of those needs and priorities that may shape your programmatic response.
- Find ways to involve community participants.
- Include elected officials, where appropriate, in a mutuality of relationship, where you hold them accountable for and to the constituencies they represent.
- Develop teams of persons to respond to emergency needs.
- Study social institutions in your community relative to their treatment of persons — in prisons, in mental hospitals, in nursing homes, and within the welfare system.
- "Give justice to the weak and the orphan; maintain the right of the lowly and the destitute. Rescue the weak and the needy; deliver them from the hand of the wicked" (Ps. 82:3–4).
- Support community action for better housing, health care, employment and child care for persons needing and receiving these services.
- Promote the understanding and acceptance of a variety of lifestyles, cultural patterns, and ethnic traditions in community, nation, and world.
- Develop clear guidelines where you make space available to other groups from your community.
- Help your congregation as a body, through planning and budgeting, to develop and support contextual ministries.

The Ministry of Jesus to Persons

Too often much of our ministry to persons with sundry needs has primarily been doing things *for* people — delivering service. But ministry is essentially *with* people. Through his interaction with people, Jesus sought to develop their understanding of God and assist persons to change their self-perception. He helped them redirect their focus away from any disabilities they had and attend more to their abilities, skills, talents, and most of all their potential as whole persons under God. He then presented them a challenge to live differently as a result of their encounter with him and in relation to the new self-discovery that they made. They turned from those encounters and witnessed to the power of God to effect transformation in their outlook and their whole way of life. The freedom they experienced through Jesus set in motion a process of empowerment in which they could think and act for themselves and on behalf of others. They could face challenges, make choices, and accept responsibilities to contribute to the transformation of life in community.

Marks of Contextually Aware Congregations

Contextually aware congregations have certain characteristics. They

- have a healthy self-awareness and understanding of themselves;
- seek to hold institutions in their contexts accountable for the welfare of all persons, particularly the poor and helpless and hopeless;
- are committed to working with other churches, agencies, and interest groups that are working for love and justice;
- live the life of faith beyond the walls and in the world;
- engage in analysis through reflection and action.

In terms of community activities and other social programs, the pastors interviewed report that their congregations are involved in many such activities. At the top of the list are youth programs (92 percent) and cash assistance to families in need (86 percent). About three-quarters are involved in food pantries or soup kitchens (75 percent) and voter registrations (76 percent). Although 45 percent of congregations are involved in social advocacy overall, AMEZ (62 percent) and blacks within United Methodist congregations (63 percent) are more likely to report this involvement. The same denominational pattern emerges regarding participation in health programs or clinics.[6]

It is interesting to note that clergy who are paid pastors, either full-time or part-time, as opposed to those who have volunteer positions, are more likely to report being involved in any of the activities and programs that were surveyed. This same pattern emerges when size of congregation is considered. The larger the congregation, the more likely it is to be involved in nearly all of the activities or programs. There are similar findings in the national profile. An additional note in this regard is that "older congregations do not differ from more recently organized groups in the number or kinds of social ministries (except that the most recently organized are less likely to be involved)."[7] "When it comes to the willingness of congregations to go beyond service and become more involved in social issue advocacy or community organizing, historically black churches rate both issues more highly than all other faith groups."[8] In the discussion on social ministry a distinction is often made between social service and social advocacy. Many congregations are readier to engage in a wide variety of ministries that provide assistance to relieve human need. This kind of activity is ongoing through many congregations. One immediately thinks of soup kitchens, homeless shelters, food banks, clothes closets, and job training. The list can be multiplied through programs that address the need of single parents, the elderly, persons battling substance abuse, and so on.

When, however, we turn our attention to social advocacy, there has not been a ready or sustained response. Congregations find it difficult to develop consensus not only about what needs to be done, but how to achieve objectives. Such advocacy is pursued, often led by individual pastors who act out of personal convictions that propel them into the public arena.

The challenge that remains for congregations and their leadership is to make the connection between an educational task and its manifestation in ministry. Further ways should be found to help persons discover the justice motif — already present in the biblical witness, both in the story of God and Israel and in the ministry of Jesus — and to explore how that becomes real in the causes espoused and programs that are developed. The degree of the ability of your congregation to respond to its community will finally rest not on the soundness of analysis, though that is important, but on the extent of your willingness to risk your own security on behalf of the insecurities of others.

Civil Rights Issues and the Black Church

The civil rights movement from the beginning was a struggle for the democratic rights guaranteed by the principles of the U.S. Constitution. Civil rights are politically defined freedoms: laws that specify what individuals and groups can do to fully participate in the society. The civil rights movement should be understood in the context of three main historical periods of African American presence in the United States — slavery, the time in the rural South, and the period in the urban North.

Lincoln and Mamiya contend that the history of the involvement of blacks in the civil rights struggle has been characterized by two traditions: the survival tradition and the liberation tradition.[9] In each of these traditions the black church has been present because there is no separation of religion and politics in the black experience.

The victory of the North over the slave system of the ante-
bellum South was consolidated in law, especially the 13th, 14th,
and 15th amendments. These amendments, along with the Bill of
Rights, established the political basis for the civil rights movement. However, the actual civil rights movement did not develop
until the twentieth century, and more particularly in the 1950s
and 1960s when blacks began consolidating in urban communities and engaged in mass action and an orientation to struggle. The
masses of black people took their demands to the streets. "The
Black Church heritage has contributed to both the survival and
liberal traditions that have shaped black attitudes towards politics.
Many of the famous historical figures in slave revolts, abolitionism,
electoral politics, and civil rights protests have either been clergy
or closely identified with black churches."[10] It is this history and
heritage that the black church must maintain in the light of contemporary situations that are to be faced as we stand at the dawn
of the new millennium.

In the total sample of black clergy, those with seminary degrees
and particularly doctoral degrees are more likely to approve of
clergy being actively involved in political action (see figure 3.1).

Naming and Framing Tensions

Black churches have a new challenge now in the light of government concerns to make funding available to support work that
churches have already been doing with limited resources. Many
black churches and pastors have responded to identified needs and
hurts of people in their communities, delivering a variety of social
services. But the complexities of the situations demand approaches
and skills for which most black pastors need preparation and
training. There needs to be an affirmation of the interrelation-
ship between social, political, and economic life. There is a definite
relationship between economics and politics. Many of the problems facing the black community are interrelated. The church must

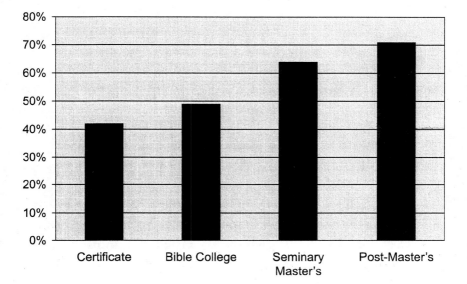

FIGURE 3.1. STRONGLY APPROVE OF CLERGY
IN PROTEST MARCHES

extend its focus beyond the history of political activism and discern that the current needs of the black community are largely economic.

There continues to be hesitancy on the part of black church leaders to be involved with government-funded programs. The fears that some pastors have expressed relate to the anxiety about financial scrutiny. This is addressed as clergy learn how to set up Community Development Corporations (CDCs) and thus prevent co-mingling of funds. More formal training is called for in economic and community development ministries and in forming partnerships with civic agencies for the common welfare of persons.

Limited funding for what the black church seeks to do for the disadvantaged continues to create somewhat irreconcilable tensions for black church leadership. The tensions include (1) whether to continue the work with limited resources or accept the resources of "Big Brother" with all of its constraints and scrutiny; (2) accept the criticism of others in the black community as a "sellout" or act as a compromised institution; (3) risk potential compromise in theological, political, or social ideology or accept economic support with the potential for constraints in these areas; and (4) extract the limited support from the membership, beg the community, seek assistance from philanthropic foundations, or partner with other unlikely groups (e.g., government agencies, churches and institutions theologically different).

Calls to march in protest are easy to make. However, in order to avail themselves of opportunities provided by the currently popular faith-based initiatives, black churches and pastors require greater preparation to navigate the systems to the benefit of the deserving. Many pastors have led congregations into ministry that makes a difference in their communities. Perhaps those pastors can be resources for others who may be interested but uninformed and hesitant. It will mean willingness on the part of those who have the knowledge to share narrative descriptions of their achievements. And beyond that they will have to offer models that answer fundamental questions, such as: What are primary steps in a process to achieve goals? Ways and models need to be found and shared to increase the number of pastors who are interested and who will respond to empowerment.

Relationship with Other Churches and Other Faiths

Natural and social disasters — hurricanes, floods, tornados, and earthquakes — have provided opportunities for cooperation among governmental agencies, churches, and other faiths. These noble efforts at working together are commendable. But there are also other widespread endemic needs such as poverty, illiteracy, unemployment, and homelessness. In our age both in our nation and in other countries in our world, HIV-AIDS demands our ongoing response as Christians. Racism, and more peculiarly institutional racism, ever present in the church, continues to rear its ugly head and is a scandal to those of us who profess and practice the Christian faith. In these and other areas of our life, action for social justice is the demand and the acid test of our love for others. Christian congregations along with other faith communities must develop ways for thinking and action to identify concrete needs and appropriate responses to them.

The church is called to work with those structures in society that are prohuman and concerned for the alleviation of human suffering and the welfare of persons. Those same systems, however, that provide for full human development also contain within them many forms of evil and suffering that result from abuse and misuse of power. Although the church cannot identify with any social, economic, or political system, members of congregations are encouraged to take an active part in the public life of their communities and nation. Political action can take many forms beyond the expression of views in the opinion pages of local newspapers. Such participation is recognition that Jesus Christ, the Sovereign of history, is at work in the world today in every nation in spite of the ambiguous social, political, and economic structures and activities in any given country, including our own. Church is the sign to the nation and the world that the last word is with God.

Checklist for Chapter 3

- Discover the variety of techniques that are used by persons in your congregation to carry out ministry.

- List the several programs (ministries) in your congregation.

- Name recent events that illustrate your congregation's participation in civil rights issues, either by individuals or by one of your auxiliaries.

Questions for Discussion, Reflection, and Action

1. What are those beliefs, religious practices, and rituals that you identify as distinctive to your denominational heritage and identity in your congregation?

2. What are some ways that your congregation prepares and plans for its several programs both within the congregation and in the community?

3. How does your congregation affirm and support its members who participate in the several outreach programs?

4. How does pastoral leadership encourage discussion and commitment to civil rights issues and social advocacy through your congregation?

LEADERSHIP AND ORGANIZATIONAL DYNAMICS

Every high priest is selected from among men and is appointed to represent them in matters related to God, to offer gifts and sacrifices for sins. He is able to deal gently with those who are ignorant and are going astray, since he himself is subject to weakness. That is why he has to offer sacrifices for his own sins, as well as for the sins of the people. No one takes this honor upon himself; he must be called by God, just as Aaron was.   — Hebrews 5:1–4 (NIV)

The clergy are being asked to identify, enlist, nurture, disciple, train, place, support, and resource teams of lay volunteers who will do the work.... This may also be the most demanding role for ministers in terms of vision, competence, creativity, leadership, dedication, strategy formulation, hard work, long hours, faithfulness, and skill in interpersonal relationships.
— Lyle E. Schaller

In this chapter you will learn about

- leadership and congregational life
- conflict, continuity, and change

- women and leadership in congregations
- spirituality and vitality in the congregation

The responsibilities of being called to Christian leadership are clear. Leaders arise from the community and are responsible to the community as bearers of the holy, a means by which the community is led into relationship with God. Leaders must also use the gifts with which they have been endowed so that the tasks of the community get done. At a deeper level, pastoral leadership derives from God and is sustained through relationship with God. The work of the minister is neither an office nor a career, but rather is a vocation and a calling. And, more importantly, our work does not separate us from others. In the fascinating phrase in Moffatt's translation of the passage from the letter to the Hebrews, "we wear the garment of human weakness." These are sobering thoughts when we would presume to judge others. We are bound up with our fellow human beings in the bundle of life. Leaders who make the inward journey to both their shadows and light can take us beyond ourselves into a needy and hurting world.

Leadership and Congregational Life

Leadership can be exercised by several persons within a congregation. Leadership is an activity by which the tasks of the congregation get done. These include, among others, enabling the congregation to gain a realistic self-understanding of its history — its particular story and the circumstances of its life; assisting the congregation to catch a vision of its life and purpose under God; and helping it to manifest its members' vision of their calling as disciples of Jesus Christ.

Effective and effectual pastoral leadership seeks to empower the congregation to be faithful to its identity as people of God and make obedient witness through its life in the community of the world.

Congregations need a pastoral leader with a deep sense of vocation, but one who is equally competent and committed to empowering others to effect transformation, through the Spirit, in their own lives and the lives of others. A good leader works with and through others to achieve goals. The persons with and through whom ministry is exercised are gifts from God to enable members to share in the ministry of their congregations.

As you seek to get work done you need to create forums where persons can talk freely and share their ideas about what they would like to see happen in their congregations and those things to which they are willing to make commitment and give their energies. Those opportunities may be informal, or you may use the structures that exist in different councils in the congregation. Their configurations and processes may vary according to a denominational culture. The perspective we would suggest is a movement away from being overly bureaucratic, programmed, and packaged from the top down. Enable team learning, where persons feel that their contributions are valued and they are assured that they can contribute to the decision-making process. Where this occurs persons will more readily accept responsibility for the sundry tasks that need to be done to fulfill your mission.

When persons participate in shaping the work to be done, they can evaluate their progress, revise their plans, make adjustments where necessary, and certainly celebrate achievements. A pastoral leader who inspires, encourages, and supports persons as they fulfill their share of the ministry will earn the trust and respect that he or she anticipates from the congregation.

On Leadership and Management

Leadership and management are two different skills. Sometimes they may reside in one person. Where they do not, they need to be recognized as complementary. Both are needed to assist your congregation to do its work. Effective leaders influence others to *think, act,* and *follow.* Perhaps one way to talk about a difference between leadership and management is to recognize how you relate to people. You show caring and quality leadership as you demonstrate a greater concern in building people rather than using them.

Dr. Henry McKinney was a staff person from the denominational office who was interested in developing a project that could enrich the life of seniors in congregations. He contacted Pastor Smith and entered into covenant with him to achieve mutually satisfying objectives. On his first visit with the pastor, Dr. McKinney requested Pastor Smith to identify a small group of persons — six in number — from the congregation with whom to work. During the welcome period at worship on Sunday morning, the pastor welcomed Dr. McKinney and shared with the congregation his interest in the project. Pastor Smith concluded his remarks by stating that six persons were needed on a team to work with Dr. McKinney on the project. He proceeded to call forth from the congregation the six persons and assigned them to the project. They all agreed. In conversation afterward, Pastor Smith confided to Dr. McKinney that the persons were ready to work on call because they recognized that the pastor was a caring person. When Sister Brown's son was in the county jail, charged with a misdemeanor, the pastor had gone to the jail with her. And when Earl Young's wife, Gloria, lingered unto death with cancer, Pastor Smith was a source of strength to him. Pastor Smith knew their several gifts and the interests of each person he had assigned, and he always had a word of support and encouragement and affirmation for their service.

As you help persons to affirm your love for them as their pastor, invest in themselves, and believe in their potential, these skills will move you away from the direction of doing things *to* people and lead you to do things *with* people. People readily submit to working with a leader who enhances and empowers others.

Calling, Character, and Conduct

As we write, the incidence of pedophilia in the Roman Catholic Church is making news daily. There have been oblique comments that sexual misconduct including pedophilia is present among clergy in other denominations, but a culture of respectable silence prevents any public confession or discussion of this matter. We have a tendency to magnify the concerns for sex and sexuality of leaders. But the totality of one's being and conduct in every area of one's life is always open to scrutiny. We are accountable for the way in which we treat others, manage the resources entrusted to us, and use our time. Are we so busy doing our work, or do we make time to find God in the center of our prayer life so that we might discern where God is present in our world and join in the work that needs to be done? The coincidence between who we are in our person and what we do imbues us with the authority to lead others. Indeed it enables us to have wholeness — integrity that makes our work acceptable to God.

> Between four and five years after my sanctification, on a certain time, an impressive silence fell upon me, and I stood as if someone was about to speak to me, yet I had no such thought in my heart. But to my utter surprise there seemed to sound a voice that I distinctly heard, and most certainly understand, which said to me, "Go preach the Gospel!" I immediately replied aloud, "No one will believe me." Again, I listened, and again the same voice seemed to say "Preach the Gospel; I will put my words in your mouth, and I will turn your enemies to become your friends."[1]

With those words, Jarena Lee describes her call to preach. It is a dramatic and fascinating story of encounter, revelation, and decision. But not all calls to preach, to ministry or service for God, come in that way. God chooses to call in different ways and under different circumstances. The biblical stories are as varied as the persons whom God called. And so has been God's call to God's servants down through the ages. But the call is always to make oneself available to God so that God's work might be done. It is always a call to work with and on behalf of God so that others may come to know, love, praise, and glorify God by the life they lead. The call is to a way of life; hence who we are in our person and what we do are important. Our work depends on our ability and our willingness to be in an ongoing relationship with the one who has called us so that we might do God's will and honor God's name.

In the Christian vocation, more than in any other leadership role, the quality and character of the person in office are important. The trilogy of relationship among *calling, character,* and *conduct* needs to be affirmed and constantly demonstrated. You may possess the ideas and the technology to meet both the intellectual and emotional challenges of leadership. Nothing, however, becomes more important than being aware of one's calling, gifts, limitations, and source of authority and power to fulfill that calling — authority derived from God and renewed by God's Holy Spirit.

The power of the Holy Spirit enables you to live in the world, as God would have you live. It is not independent of the disciplines that may follow or the mastery of skills that you can acquire. Essentially it comes from turning to God.

Some Characteristics of Effective Leaders

Leaders possess the following qualities, among others:

- An effective leader must exhibit *integrity* in his or her person and be able to inspire and call it forth in others.

- *Trust* and *mutual respect* develop morale and encourage high productivity. An effective leader, therefore, must prove to be trustworthy.

- Effective leaders are visionaries who have the capacity to articulate clear visions to which they and others can respond.

- Effective leaders are *self-motivated* and can inspire others to action through their own commitment to a mission and their dedication to high standards of excellence.

- An effective leader needs a sense of *humor*. It helps to relieve tension. Humor, humility, human — all the words have the same Latin root: *humus*. It means of the earth, ground, thus, earthy, down to earth; it also suggests that one is like others, who are equally of the earth. Thus effective leaders have a capacity to laugh at themselves and can be compassionate with the mistakes of others. (If the baboon could see his behind, he would laugh too [Swahili proverb].)

- Effective leaders are *dependable*. They can be relied upon to keep commitments and follow through.

- The effective leader always keeps an *open mind*, open to possibilities beyond what her or his limited, finite mind can imagine. He or she is prepared to look at situations from other angles of vision.

The list of characteristics that we have offered above is not meant in any way to be definitive or exhaustive. Rather it is an invitation to self-reflection and self-evaluation. You may also be similarly engaged.

Shared Leadership

An Akan proverb states, "If you say you know everything, you will sleep in the hallway of fools." No one of us has all that it takes to work for God. We need others and others need us. The days of the pastoral leader who has all the ideas, makes all the decisions, and can do all that needs to be done are past. Perhaps there never was such a time. The recognition of this reality has come home sharply to those who lead congregations. There is a paradigm shift in the leadership of congregations. The role of pastoral leader is to free up the laity for greater responsibilities. The kind of leadership that will empower congregations in mission and for ministry is transforming leadership:

> The transforming leader is critically involved in envision-
> ing, communicating and creating an improved future for self,
> any other person, group or organization.... The transform-
> ing leader also has a well-defined sense of mission, purpose,
> values, goals, and strategies which are based upon a deep
> understanding of people and the aims which are being served,
> and a clear understanding of the cultural, political and eco-
> nomic environment surrounding the change endeavor being
> attempted."[2]

All of this means that pastors must be open to, nurture, and prepare persons for shared leadership, to become partners in ministry for the several tasks that need to be done so that congregations can fulfill their mission in church and world.

In Need of More and Better-Educated Pastoral Leaders

Our research has shown leaders of the churches studied had the following level of ministerial education: post–master of divinity work or degree (30 percent), Bible college or some seminary (26 percent), seminary degree (24 percent), and none (9 percent).[3] Only 4 percent reported an apprenticeship and 3 percent a certificate or correspondence program. Pastors of black Presbyterian and black United Methodist churches were more likely than pastors of the five remaining denominations to have a post–master of divinity or doctor of ministry degree. COGIC pastors were least likely to report any formal ministerial training. The mean age of the pastors of the congregations interviewed was fifty-five and most pastors (96 percent) were male.

The picture among African American pastors described above accords with the national profile as painted by the larger study of congregational life in the United States, where data from our Project 2000 is also included. The following observation is very noteworthy in light of the last item mentioned concerning the age of black pastors:

> Aging leadership affects every group, but the challenge is particularly pronounced in some groups. Indeed, the average religious leader of Catholic/Orthodox and historically black denominations is less than a decade away from the typical retirement age of 65, while the Evangelical Protestant and World groups' leaders have 50 percent more time until they reach 65.[4]

Growing Leaders from within the Community of Faith

A concern that faces African American congregations is nurturing, growing, and recruiting pastoral leaders. One of the ways that the faith has taken root among a people is the emergence from their ranks of leaders that can identify and call their own. This occurs as congregations create conditions of nurture in faith development and the kind of spiritual development in which persons can hear and discern the call of God. Each of us tells his or her own story. Paul reminds the Corinthians to recall the kinds of persons they were when God called them:

> Not many were wise by human standards; not many were powerful, not many were of noble birth. But God chose what is foolish in the world to shame the wise; God chose what is weak in the world to shame the strong; God chose what is low and despised in the world, the things that are not, to reduce to nothing things that are, so that no one might boast in the presence God. He is the source of your life in Christ Jesus, who has become for us wisdom from God, and righteousness and

sanctification and redemption, in order that, as it is written, "Let the one who boasts boast in the Lord" (1 Cor. 1:26–31).

It is in this context of nurture in the community of faith that persons can be affirmed and made open to discern the claim of God on their lives and hear a call to ministry. As you and your congregation are open to cultivating persons, God can use the Holy Spirit in the congregation to renew and resource the church for building up the body of Christ and bringing the reign of God nearer.

Identifying, Managing, and Sharing Gifts

Everybody knew Eloise for the fried chicken that she prepared for the Sunday fellowship meal after morning worship. They wouldn't have missed it for the world, as they say. The demand was so great that many persons went away disappointed because there never seemed to be enough. Then somebody thought to learn more about this person — Eloise. They learned that she was a qualified accountant — a CPA. She was subsequently invited and committed to making her knowledge and services available on the finance committee.

People are your primary resource as you seek to lead a congregation in fulfilling its vocation as the people of God. You need to develop a list of persons and a process for identifying gifts and personal interests. Sundry resources are available for such a bank of resources. However, you may develop your own. A data-gathering instrument can identify the tasks that the congregation needs to have done. At the same time, you may write job descriptions. Establish a human resources bank. Become aware of opportunities for service. Seek to match gifts to tasks. Provide training opportunities. Develop long-range plans. Establish growth groups in which persons reflect on their commitment and involvement and seek ways to renew themselves for continuing engagement in service to others.

At Glendale, the pastor, Dr. Henson, silenced Sister Jessie Thomas as she attempted to contribute to the discussion on the church's budget. Sister Jessie tried to make sure that responsible use was being made of the church's resources. She was director of budget and management in city government. Pastor Henson had appointed her to the church finance committee. Now he was dismissing what she had to say, declaring that he was in charge and that his actions were not to be questioned. Regrettably, because of the pastor's attitude, Sister Jessie withdrew from the committee and the membership of that congregation. We need to find ways not only for identifying and managing the varied gifts of members, but also affirming them as they make those gifts available in the congregation. To this end, pastoral leaders are challenged to affirm and empower persons to use their gifts for the benefit of the common ministry entrusted to the congregation.

Conflict, Continuity, and Change in Congregational Life

The women's auxiliary at Mount Pleasant always held their anniversary dinner on the fourth Sunday in May. This event was begun under the leadership of Sister Ouida James over twenty years ago. Everyone in the congregation looked forward to it. It was considered *the* social event of parish life. The youth fellowship, a much younger organization, was growing in numbers. Their initial efforts were faltering and hesitant. But ever since Victor Johnson took over the leadership of the group, his infectious enthusiasm was attracting more youth into the group. Under his leadership, young people felt that they found a place where they were affirmed and their voice was heard, and they could shape plans for events that were to their benefit and that Victor Johnson could support. Then they planned a fashion show for the same day the women's auxiliary had selected for its dinner.

Conflict arises when we seek to make choices. As individuals, we have conflicts when we must make the choice to be one place or another. We can describe that as intrapersonal conflict. Where such a situation is present within a group, we can think of it as an intergroup conflict. This is what occurred at Mount Pleasant. An intergroup conflict had arisen. It was created by legitimate and competing claims between the women's auxiliary and the youth fellowship. Conflict will always be present where persons gather in community. Each of us is different from one another. We have different ways of looking at things. We bring to any circumstance the persons we are, with our knowledge, our experiences, and our beliefs.

Our life together in congregations mirrors our life in other encounters. Conflict then is part of common life. It occurs whenever persons fail to agree on anything. We begin to deal with it as we recognize that we have differences. How we deal with it and what use we make of it will determine the quality of our ongoing life together. Church groups and leaders tend to handle conflict poorly. Persons harbor resentments, sometimes holding on to unpleasant encounters for many years. They are unwilling to let go and be reconciled. The beginning of the process of resolving conflict is the willingness to let go. The willingness to let go opens the way for forgiveness and reconciliation. Yet if we use creativity in our approach the energy we invest in attempting to resolve conflict will pay dividends for all concerned.

Congregations, like all living organizations, experience change. New persons join our fellowship; the practices and rituals we follow sometimes become outmoded. Decisions are made to change, to respond to new conditions and circumstances. What shall we retain? What are those things that we need to get rid of? How do we mediate between competing claims? How do we help persons in conflict achieve resolution with dignity and mutual satisfaction?

Change in pastoral leadership can sometimes be difficult for congregations. Much of that anxiety can be reduced or eliminated where leaders recognize the role they have in empowering persons to reexamine and claim their story, discover and accept their shared beliefs and values, and be open to the possibilities that can move them to deeper levels of their common life. It is equally important that both the pastor who is moving and the one who is coming in anticipate problems and plan and carry out change in that situation, as in others, with strategies that foster outcomes for the good of the congregation. Change can provide opportunities not only for rebuilding, but for renewing commitment that can structure growth.

The issues of conflict, continuity, and change are interrelated. Congregations that are willing to recognize the conflict and enable the parties to deal with the issues have the capacity for vitality and growth. This is another opportunity where you can utilize the human relations skills of members already trained in this field to serve as an internal facilitator in the process. If you determine that the situation is so grave that it cannot be dealt with, you may wish to consider engaging the services of an external consultant.

Women and Leadership of Congregations

The issue that is most divergent by denomination is approval of a woman as pastor of a church. On the one hand, 40 percent of clergy strongly approve, while only 20 percent of Baptists and 23 percent of COGIC strongly approve. On the other hand, one in ten clergy members of the remaining denominations strongly approve of women as pastors of their own church. Methodist denominations report between 77 and 88 percent who are ready to receive a woman as pastor.[5]

At breakfast one morning at a regional conference of ministers, one woman shared with us an experience that she claimed was disappointing to her. She had recently been in attendance at a Bible college where women were denied enrollment in preaching classes. It was the position of that particular school that women had no place in the pulpit. This denial of affirmation of women's ability to serve God in any and all roles in which God uses persons is not new. Jarena Lee, who is believed to be the first woman licensed to preach in the African Methodist Episcopal Church, makes the case in her journal for her right, as a woman, to preach. She writes: "If the man may preach, because the saviour died for him, why not a woman? Seeing he died for her also. Is he not a whole saviour, instead of a half one? As those who hold it wrong for a woman to preach, would seem to make it appear."[6]

Women have continued in every available forum to raise their voices for legitimate leadership roles in the church. The pressure of their claim has been articulated, impassioned, and insistent. But their leadership roles are still limited in many African American congregations. The lack of access to the pulpit is only one manifestation of the problem. Women are grudgingly placed on deacon and trustee boards as members. Their presence is carefully limited and managed so that election to leadership as chairperson is rare. An even greater and more pressing concern is the affirmation and acceptance of women in pastoral leadership. Yet it is only as churches, and more particularly African American denominations, permit honest and open discussion at every level that their potential for growth will be realized.

In such a discussion, the old and tired arguments should not be rehearsed: that God does not call women to preach or lead congregations; that a woman could be an evangelist but not a pastor. Additionally, an educational approach as proposed would seek to change the attitudes of persons — demonstrating that women are liberated to affirm that God's gifts do not come gender-assigned and limited to men. This needs to be a continuing education experience where the contributions that women have made and can make will be affirmed and redound to the enrichment of the life of all persons in congregations.

Black Women in Church and Society: An Imaginative Response

The office of Black Women in Church and Society[7] was organized in 1981 at the Interdenominational Theological Center. It began as a vision of Dr. Jacquelyn Grant, a professor of systematic theology whose groundbreaking work in womanist theology has made her well known not only in the United States but around the world. She has a passionate commitment to empowering women in ministry and has pursued this interest with much imagination and creativity. The Black Women in Church and Society initiative has spawned a number of programs that express its goal of increasing the knowledge base about black women in the church and society, seeking to correct misconceptions about African American women and advance their cause for full participation in church and society.

A number of programs and activities have been developed over the years of its existence. These have included courses in the theological curriculum at ITC and informal dialogues that bring men and women together in sensitizing conversations aimed at deepening understanding between the sexes. A most recent conversation explored the role of the church in recognizing and responding to partner violence and sexual assault, with emphasis on theology and praxis. The whole community at ITC, the larger community in Atlanta, and particularly higher education have benefited from the Womanist Scholars Program. Womanist scholars in several disciplines have pursued their research, taught courses, and enhanced our appreciation of the signal contributions of black women in all areas of our common life. Through funding from the Ford Foundation, an internship program has helped forge alliances between clergy and social service agencies. These experiences have proved mutually beneficial — the agencies and their workers obtain services while interns develop skills and are prepared for leadership roles. A new component on black women in leadership development is being planned and will offer positions in leadership and leadership development within the church and community. This program initiative is a significant center for empowering and eminently preparing women for many roles, including pastoral leadership of congregations.

Pastor Stewart's Tale

On March 4, 1995, Christ Missionary Baptist Church, where Rev. Stewart was reared, nurtured, and developed for spiritual maturity, took a tremendous "leap of faith," stepped outside of its denominational tradition, and elected a female to serve as its pastor. The Rev. Gina M. Stewart was elected by majority vote and became the first African American female elected to serve an established Baptist church in Memphis and Shelby County. Pastor Stewart became the second pastor of Christ Missionary Baptist Church, following the sudden and untimely death in May 1994 of her predecessor and mentor, the Rev. Eddie L. Currie, who had served for twenty-seven years.

Despite predictions of failure and speculation that the election of Rev. Stewart would result in a church split, the church has grown from approximately four hundred members to more than eighteen hundred. In October 2001, the church broke ground for a $3.5 million worship center with seating for fifteen hundred. In May 2001, the church ordained four women as deacons for the first time in the church's history.

In addition to embracing a new paradigm of leadership with a female at its helm, the church embraces a comprehensive commitment to producing indefatigable imitators of Christ who live God-honoring lives as "change agents" in our culture.

As she looks to the future, Pastor Stewart reflects, "The past seven years have been challenging, trying, and rewarding. In many

FIGURE 4.1. APPROVAL OF WOMEN AS PASTORS

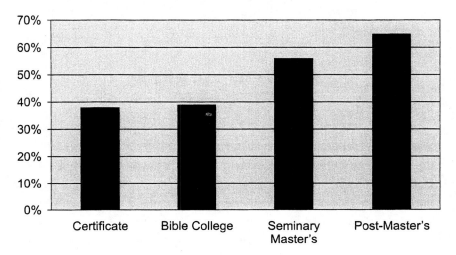

ways, we have seen and experienced the miraculous. It is my prayer that God will do even greater works as God is invited and allowed to do so."[8]

It is interesting to note, as figure 4.1 from our research shows, that in the total sample of black clergy, the better educated the pastors, the more favorable they are toward women pastors.[9]

Cheryl Townsend Gilkes has contended that " 'If it wasn't for the women,' the black community would not have had the churches and other organizations that have fostered the psychic and material survival of individuals and that have mobilized the constituencies that have produced change and progress."[10] The issue is one that African American denominations can no longer treat casually and tentatively. Delores Carpenter's *A Time for Honor*[11] calls for us to recognize and honor clergywomen who are being eminently qualified for all aspects of leadership and ministry in churches. She has carefully documented claims that cannot be denied. Denominations must therefore confront and address, with seriousness and creativity, the issue of women in pastoral leadership. The gifts, talents, skills, and dedication that women have to offer can only continue to enhance and increase the health and vitality of congregational life.

Spirituality and Vitality in Congregational Life

The Sunday morning began at Mount Moriah when the pastor, who was also a musician, went to the piano and struck chords that led the congregation in the popular hymn: "This Is the Day That the Lord Has Made." They slowly picked up the cues. Pastor Brockton had been at Mount Moriah for nearly a decade. They knew him and he knew them. So when he suggested that they could do better than that, they understood where he was coming from. He continued, "Every day is the Lord's day. Let's give God some praise for this day that God had given us." The congregation responded; they got the message. Perhaps the Spirit started to descend at Mount Moriah and began to move among the saints. The music got louder and the sanctuary began to vibrate. The session went on for the next twenty minutes. Spiritual vitality is often perceived as exciting and inspiring a movement in which the whole congregation participates and the preacher's ability evokes "Amens" and much applause.

In the church described in Acts 2 there was oneness of heart and mind and spirit — and it grew, as God added daily to their number. Numerical growth is related to the growth of members in their deepening relationship with God through the Holy Spirit. An examination of the story of Pentecost raises several questions for self-evaluation of the life in your congregation. Do you encourage your members to engage in daily devotions in which they seek to be in God's presence and open to the Spirit in their lives? Are there opportunities where members discover and share their experiences with God with one another? Do the worship experiences in your congregation lead members to move from worship to service with and to others in community? How does the life of the Spirit within one's life become real in one's life in the world?

Spiritual vitality is fundamentally life, energy, and *power* that come from the Spirit. It is interesting to note that the Greek word used in Acts for the power that the Spirit gives is the word from which our English words "dynamic" and "dynamite" are derived. It is the Spirit that gives energy and power to effect change and transformation not only in one's self, but also in congregational life.

For our physical health, we are advised to have an occasional or, as we grow older, a regular medical check-up. You make an appointment with your primary physician and undergo a battery of tests. Then an opinion is given of the state of your health. If any disease is found, you are told what you should do. As individuals, it is good for us to have a spiritual "check-up." You can take a couple hours in this examination, and it's not expensive. Actually all that it will cost you is honesty with yourself. You can look at your life in the world, your life at home, your life in church, how you use your resources — your time, your gifts, and your treasure. Most importantly, you need to examine your relationship to and your service for Jesus Christ.

Similarly, you can lead your congregation in an examination of its life in the Spirit. It is so easy for a congregation to keep on doing the same things week after week, so that their life becomes routine and unexciting. Some of the questions in such a spiritual check-up might include: Why do we exist as a congregation? What if our church were to close its doors today, who would miss it and why? What is our church doing for those who don't attend worship and are disaffected for one reason or another? Other questions could be developed.

We wish to offer one way to evaluate and promote spiritual vitality in congregational life. Other or different lists could be found or suggested. Spiritually vital congregations have groups in which persons have a sense of belonging and are regularly exploring the meaning of their faith and mutually supporting one another. They find and create places for persons to discover and use their gifts and skills to assist the congregation to fulfill its mission and engage in meaningful ministry. Through the disciplines of prayer and Bible study in private and public worship persons experience relationship with God. Spiritually vital congregations enable persons in a variety of ways to find and make connections between their faith and daily life. Consistent with our perspective in this book, we are not offering prescriptions that if followed faithfully would guarantee vitality. The Spirit blows where it wills. There are many resources that are available to assist if you wish to lead your congregation into spiritual vitality or renewal of its life, seeking to fulfill its mission for God. If you are open to the Spirit, you will be led into a future that God directs and that gives shape to congregational life that only glorifies God.

From our research that yielded a national profile of congregational life, the overall view of black pastors of predominantly black congregations at the beginning of the new millennium is that their congregations are spiritually alive and they are excited about the future.

Checklist for Chapter 4

- Determine the nature and level of conflict that exists in your congregation and decide what steps you need to take to effect resolution.

- Invite groups in your congregation to explore ways and make specific suggestions for affirming and supporting women in roles of pastoral leadership.

- Plan and carry out an evaluation of your congregational life.

- Decide on a time, theme, and place for your congregational retreat.

Questions for Discussion, Reflection, and Action

1. In what ways does pastoral leadership foster or frustrate a sense of community in this congregation?

2. What are some ways that congregations can create more opportunities for persons to hear and respond to the call of God for full-time service?

3. How are those who exercise leadership roles recruited, assigned, affirmed, supported, and nurtured?

4. What role does leadership play in shaping and embodying the vision(s) for ministry of the congregation?

5. What connections are evident between character and competence in the selection and exercise of leadership?

~ *Five* ~

FINANCES

The earth is the Lord's and all that is in it, the world, and those
who live in it.   —Psalm 24:1

I have discovered in life that there are ways of getting almost
anywhere you want to go, if you really want to go.
                                                    —Langston Hughes

In this chapter you will explore aspects of

- financial stewardship

- working with volunteers

There are few themes more central to biblical literature than the
sovereignty of God. It is a concept rooted in creation and elabo-
rated in historical experience. Psalm 24:1 is one of the central texts
for understanding the breadth and the significance of this concept;
the sovereignty of God is not merely a religious affirmation—it is a
basis of worship and praise. Those who worship are those who recognize the sovereignty, who accept the rule of the supreme God. The
genius of this psalm lies in the way it links cosmological belief and
historical experience. From the perspective of cosmology, the world
is created and thus represents order; God established that order.
But historical experience, often characterized by conflict, suggests
a different reality, namely, that the world is marked by chaos.

Few topics bring as much conflict and chaos to congregational life as that of finances. Money is a complicated symbol psychologically, and it is bound up with a daunting range of theological themes.[1] While the psalm above certainly does not reflect chaos related to finances, it was deliberately chosen for the powerful language it evokes. If the earth and all that is in it is God's, and the world and those who live in it are stewards of God's gifts, then every member of the church must submit to the sovereignty of Christ over their own life and Christ's headship over the church. Thus, all our money and possessions and our very lives belong to God.

Financial Stewardship

The basic mission of the church today has not changed from that of the first century — it is to evangelize, equip, and care for the flock. Unfortunately, the level of resources available to many churches now doesn't differ very much from the level of resources available to first-century churches.

Christian stewardship involves all aspects of life and all uses of money. One of the most confusing concepts within financial stewardship is tithing.

Many churches interpret the teaching on tithing to mean that you should give 10 percent of your money to the church. However, Jesus is purported to have said: "Woe to you scribes and Pharisees, hypocrites! For you tithe mint, dill and cumin, and have neglected the weighty matters of the law, justice and mercy and faith. It is these you ought to have practiced without neglecting the others. You blind guides! You strain at a gnat and swallow a camel!" (see Matt. 23).

A deeper understanding of tithing, therefore, is that you give 10 percent of all that you have to God — not just in terms of money, but 10 percent of your time, your efforts, your energy, and your feelings. This is where the idea of spiritual practices comes in. You dedicate certain efforts toward serving, growing, and opening up to God and to your own highest good, which is also the good of all.

Tithing generally refers to the mechanics of giving to the church and other causes. Christians believe that the nature of God furnishes the ultimate basis for giving, that the motive for giving is more important than the amount donated, and that all Christians should give cheerfully, sacrificially, and systematically. Discussions about tithing generally are polarized around two perspectives: whether tithing continues to be binding on contemporary Christians and whether the Bible authoritatively sanctions tithing.

Defenders of tithing argue that it was commanded in the Hebrew Scriptures and was not rescinded in the Christian Scriptures. Jesus, in fact, endorsed tithing because it was vitally necessary to both individual spiritual growth and the advancement of God's reign. Moreover, the principle of God's ownership of all things has been widely practiced in church history. Congregations that use tithing plans, advocates contend, engage in aggressive local missionary work, support foreign missions, experience revivals, add many new members, arouse great interest in the community, develop a spirit of cooperation and harmony, abolish their debts, pay their pastors well, and demonstrate the power of the Holy Spirit.

Tithing advocates also allege that many tithers enjoy business success, personal prosperity, and the spiritual benefits of great joy and future treasure in heaven. Malachi 3:10–11 and Proverbs 3:9–10 are often cited as biblical "proofs" that tithing absolutely guarantees material blessings.

While acknowledging that tithing has produced many good results, other church leaders counter that tithing was not authoritatively sanctioned in the Bible and thus could not properly be said to be *the* biblical standard for giving. To require tithing is to mandate legalism in the church, which is contrary to the Spirit of Christ and the principle of grace.[2] Furthermore, tithing could too easily become a substitute for the proper management of all possessions. In fact, it can be argued that giving should be proportionate to people's means. Tithing, the giving of 10 percent of one's possessions to the church, may be too much for some, and for others, it may be too little. In fact, neither Jesus nor Paul said anything about tithing. Paul simply instructed individuals to give as God had prospered them. People must decide individually how much to give in proportion to their income, whether it is 5 percent or 50 percent. The issue for tithing is the practice of stewardship by recognizing God's lordship over all life and our responsibility to use wisely and creatively all the resources God has entrusted to us to develop God's realm.

In a discussion with representatives from four of the seven denominations that participated in the Project 2000 survey on historically black denominations, the question of finances evoked very passionate conversation. Participants sought to discover the criteria that were used for determining financial health. There was a general sentiment that the profile we developed did not represent the reality in a majority of congregations. As these church leaders reviewed questions that were asked in the survey, we discovered a number of variables that could reflect how the question of financial health could have been misconstrued.[3] One such variable was that some congregations do not operate with a budget. Others operate with an expense budget that is largely concerned with maintenance — paying for utilities, minor repairs — and an undue anxiety about meeting assessments for the general church. These church leaders expressed frustration that there was hardly any money available for outreach or missionary work. Still other church leaders felt that our data did not factor into the equation pastoral compensation, as many pastors are part-time or bi-vocational.

This discussion among pastors and church leaders is typical of conversations we have had in numerous churches. Each time, pastors and other church leaders challenged us to come up with some answers. But as we said in the introduction, this book is about helping congregations discover their identity as a community of faith, improve their capacity for meaningful ministry, and identify resources available to them. To that end, chapter 5 will focus on two aspects of financial health of black churches: (1) spiritual foundations for financial management and (2) financial health, church size, and growth.

Financial Health

A majority of the full sample of black churches surveyed reported being financially stable. It seems that only a small percentage of black congregations feel they are in serious financial difficulty (see figure 5.1) This is good news. The bad news is that many congregations we spoke to in the process of disseminating research findings disagreed with the financial conclusions of the research. What's a congregation to do?

FIGURE 5.1. FINANCIAL HEALTH

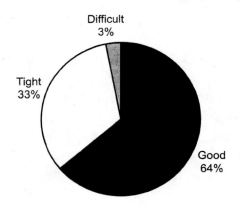

Difficult 3%

Tight 33%

Good 64%

Two Rules for Congregations

There are two key rules for congregations. The first rule is: mission, mission, mission! The second rule, which is the focus of the remaining portion of this chapter, is: no money, no mission.

In the following pages we will provide principles and guidance to pastoral and congregational leadership for both large and small congregations related to being good stewards of God's gifts. The principles are derived from our research, many years of consulting with congregational leaders, and real-world experiences in church settings.

A Spiritual Look at Financial Management

Wouldn't it be nice if we could look in the Bible and find a guide for operating church finances? In many respects the Bible is silent on church finances. It does not talk about budgets, finance committees, or financial reports. However, it does outline a support system through tithes and offerings (Mal. 3:6–12); develops a financial decision-making system (Acts 6:1–7; 15:1–19); and talks about a corrupt church treasurer (John 12:4–6). The Bible also talks to church members about spending their money (e.g., caring for the poor and supporting pastors).

Matthew 25:14–30 is the parable of talents (talents were units of money in the time of Jesus). In this parable, a master gives each of three servants some money, which he expects them to invest and give an accounting for when he returns. The first two double their money, but the third servant buries his money. The master calls him a wicked, lazy servant for doing so.

Many people understand this parable incorrectly, saying that God gives everyone inborn gifts and, in turn, everyone gives God an account of what they did with them. But if the parable's main point is not about special abilities, then what is the point? It's a lesson for both the church and its members on handling money.

First, the parable shows that God (the master) is the source of money. Second, the parable teaches that the church treasury is not a place to build wealth. It is simply a pipeline through which God funnels wealth to care for the poor, advance the gospel, and otherwise take care of the church. Third, the parable teaches about a grand accounting. During this accounting, all people will report on what they did with the money they were given. When God gives your church resources, people, or assignments to develop, God expects faithful stewardship. Jesus sums up this principle in this way: If you are faithful in a little, God will make you ruler over much (see Matt. 25:21)

How Do Black Congregations Support Their Churches?

In 1997, the Institute of Church Administration and Management (ICAM) located within the Interdenominational Theological Center conducted a national survey of African American church giving. They reported that after considering many organizational, environmental, and individual members' factors, those that were most associated with giving in the black church included the church members' age, income, spirituality, and religiosity; whether the member held a position within the church; the denomination; and how well the church managed its financial affairs. What seemed to motivate the African American church members to give to their respective houses of worship was their spirituality and commitment to keep God's covenant to support the church. Whereas the actual amount given was largely determined by the member's income. The analysis revealed a number of interesting observations about the church in the African American experience. Several recommendations emanated from the survey that may be useful to African American clergy and lay leaders:

- Many local churches did not have adequate demographic information about their members.

- Formal programs about stewardship, tithing, or use of God's gifts were not a part of many churches.

- It is difficult for churches to take on further responsibility in helping the growing number of needy.

- Expanding outreach ministries may be most effectively addressed ecumenically.

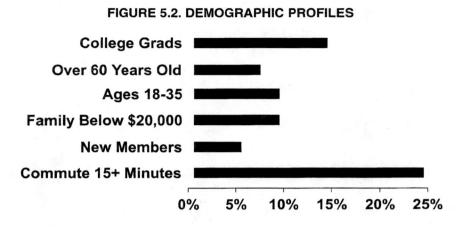

FIGURE 5.2. DEMOGRAPHIC PROFILES

We examined several aspects of demographic profiles related to the black church (see figure 5.2). As part of your congregational study, having similar knowledge of each component will help you improve your capacity for engaging in meaningful ministry.

Characteristics of Actively Participating Adults

Characteristics of members in the seven historically black churches studied were similar, with slight variations, to those in some of the categories within denominations. Figure 5.3 reflects the variations.

Information related to the demographics of your congregation will help you identify areas on which you may want to focus your ministry programs or areas in which you want to develop new ministries. Figures 5.4, 5.5, and 5.6 represent the Baptist denomination. We found that there was actually wide variance among the

FIGURE 5.3. DEMOGRAPHIC PROFILES BY DENOMINATION

	AME	AMEZ	Baptist	CME	COGIC	UMC	Pres.
College Grads	20%	21%	10%	16%	5%	28%	40%
Over 60 Years Old	9%	10%	5%	9%	3%	14%	9%
Ages 18–35	8%	5%	9%	9%	12%	5%	7%
Family Below $20,000	7%	9%	6%	15%	12%	4%	3%
New Members	5%	6%	5%	5%	6%	2%	1%
Commute 15+ min.	24%	25%	22%	24%	25%	26%	26%

FIGURE 5.4. BAPTIST DISTRIBUTION OF MEMBER CHARACTERISTICS (RURAL)

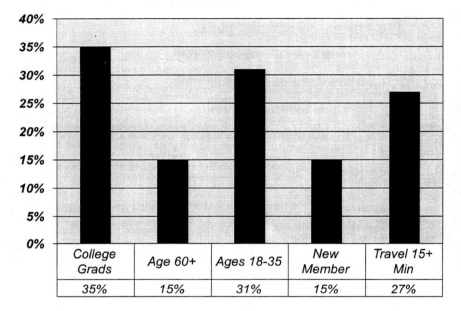

College Grads	Age 60+	Ages 18-35	New Member	Travel 15+ Min
35%	15%	31%	15%	27%

seven historically black denominations we studied. For example, in rural Presbyterian churches, 73 percent of the members were college graduates. Yet in the COGIC denomination, only 10 percent of rural members were college graduates. In the CME denomination, 62 percent of urban members traveled over fifteen minutes to church, and in the AMEZ denomination, 60 percent of members traveled fifteen or more minutes to their churches. For a complete set of denominational charts by rural-urban-suburban location, see appendix B.

What Is the Best Financial System for Churches?

Churches have distinct natures. Some churches want members to be a part of every decision. These churches need a financial system that allows for input from the members. Other congregations

**FIGURE 5.5. BAPTIST DISTRIBUTION OF MEMBER
CHARACTERISTICS (URBAN)**

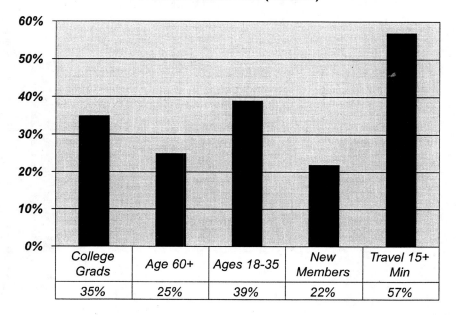

College Grads	Age 60+	Ages 18-35	New Members	Travel 15+ Min
35%	25%	39%	22%	57%

want church leadership to do everything. These churches need a financial system that focuses on the church board. Additionally, different types of pastors' needs may require different types of financial systems. Some pastors like involvement in the church's money decisions; other do not. Some pastors are naive about finances; others have strong financial backgrounds. As you explore the system your congregation either has or needs to develop, it is important to define your situation and review it periodically. Your congregation needs to tailor a financial system to meet your needs, and your needs will certainly change over the years.

All this sounds good, but how does one design a financial system that works? Unfortunately, there is no one system that is right for every church. The financial system you set for your church depends on your church and on you. The financial system for a

FIGURE 5.6. BAPTIST DISTRIBUTION OF MEMBER CHARACTERISTICS (SUBURBAN)

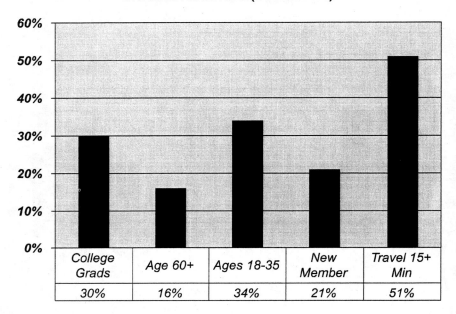

College Grads	Age 60+	Ages 18-35	New Member	Travel 15+ Min
30%	16%	34%	21%	51%

two-thousand-member church is not like the system for a two-hundred-member church or a twenty-member church. Each church has many systems that organize how things will get done. Sometimes these systems are formal (written down); sometimes they are informal ("everybody knows Sarah keeps track of who is sick"). In many churches these systems evolve with need, but more often churches end up with all sorts of systems that do not work in unity. No matter how big or small a church is, no matter what its nature, and no matter what its mission — every system in your congregation should have these features: planning, organization, direction, and control.

We know that there is a tendency within congregations to focus on faith. This is right and proper. A focus on faith will lead to understanding our call to minister to the congregation and help those in need in the community. Helping those in need sometimes makes us push for more mission before the money is there. "If it's not in the budget, that's okay. This is a real need. God will provide." When I hear this, I am always reminded of a minister friend whose response to this statement is: "I, too, believe that God will provide. But after many years in the ministry, I've learned that God's timing with money is different than mine."

So how do we balance mission and money? How do congregations raise, budget, use, and account for every nickel on financial issues at the expense of all other issues the congregation has? Finding the balance between mission and money is what your congregation may require. Use the guidelines presented here to see if all the systems in your church are working in balance.

Seeking Balance between Mission and Money

Churches often fall into two extremes: those that are obsessed with their financial issues and those that have little control over their finances. The first type has many meetings, has rigorous financial controls, and is controlled by its finances. The other type has a budget in name only. The financial reporting is inconsistent and sometimes even inaccurate. Probably there is no financial committee; there are only informal financial policies (or ones terribly outdated and usually ignored); and there may or may not be an annual audit. Does either of these organizations sound even partially familiar? If so, your congregation is at risk of not attending to its financial house.

Planning

"All we do in this church is have meetings — budget meetings, nominating meetings, board meetings. We are always meeting." This church has plenty of meetings, but it lacks direction; it needs an overall sense of mission and purpose. Building purpose truly

FIGURE 5.7. DEMOGRAPHIC PROFILES

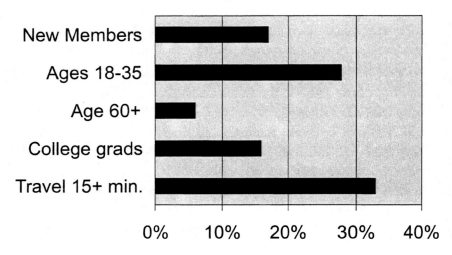

requires the grace of God. One way to build purpose is creating a congregational mission statement.

If your congregation has a mission statement, use it to review every program, expense, fund-raising activity, and other decision. Abandon everything that does not agree with the mission statement — or else change the mission statement. Congregations change over time. Mission statements or things that your congregation focused on over time have probably been affected by the change in your membership demographics. Look at figure 5.7 to see the pattern of change that was recently found in congregational demographics. Determining if your congregation follows this same pattern or a different one will help you with planning for the future.

Distribution of Member Characteristics of Churches Organized 1966–2000

Some churches see planning as wrong. They believe sooner or later the Holy Spirit will show them what to do. Good stewardship demands careful planning: assessment of what your community wants and needs, looking at your congregational strengths and weaknesses in meeting those needs and wants, and figuring how best to focus your resources to get the most mission out of your congregation. Remember, the first rule of congregations is mission, mission, mission!

If a congregation does not know where it is going, the only way you get anywhere is by accident. What you do is much, much too important to be accidental. So putting some time and effort into developing plans for your congregation make sense, makes good use of your resources, and exemplifies your responsibilities as stewards.

Another misconception about planning is that it restricts you. "If we have a plan, then we have to follow it. What if the situation changes? We're stuck." Of course the situation will change; it always does. *The idea of planning does not restrict you but allows you to focus your organization on what you think is most important.* When you are planning, build on your church's strengths, not its weaknesses. Just as people have different spiritual gifts, different churches have different gifts. Some churches do not do anything well because they try to do everything. Do not let your planning sessions digress into what the church ought to be doing but is not. When you are looking at the church's mission, focus on the church's strong points and add no more than one or two new programs.

Why Do We Need a Mission Statement?

Who are you as a congregation? Why do you exist? What do you do? Whom do you serve? Anyone coming into contact with your congregation has these questions. A mission statement should provide the answers. Many mission statements read like the Great Commission: " . . . to spread the Gospel to the people of the world." There is nothing wrong with that. However, sooner or later the high-sounding mission statement must be broken down into workable goals.

A mission statement should include three things:

- *purpose:* one sentence that describes the end result your congregation seeks to accomplish (and for whom);
- *means:* a description of the primary means (programs, services, etc.) used to accomplish the purpose;
- *values:* a list of values and beliefs or guiding principles shared by members of an organization and practiced in their work.

St. James UMC worked several months developing its mission statement, which is: "Our mission is to help people grow in faith that translates belief into action." Its mission statement is posted in every room of its facilities. Every person who comes in the doors knows what this church believes and expects from its members. After your congregation has found its mission, set its goals, and made plans for reaching those goals, it is ready for the next step: organizing.

Structure

A church's structure is the way it works on its goals. Churches' structures are as varied as their goals. Generally though, churches are divided into segments: the parts of the organizational structure that do certain things or serve certain groups. For example, a Sunday school director communicates to all Sunday school teachers. Since a church's structure governs how a church handles its finances, part of your congregational study should identify your church structure along with the strengths and weaknesses imbedded in the organization of your congregation.

Most churches organize by function: Sunday school, youth programs, women's and men's groups, outreach programs, music department, worship committee, and so on. Jobs are usually well defined within each function. But as churches grow, function-based structures start to show weaknesses. For example, the music director may plan a concert the same day as the women's group plans a marriage retreat. The larger the church, the more these problems occur.

To deal with such problems, some churches organize around the people it serves. This is called a program structure. It too has problems. Jobs are not as clearly defined as in the function-based structure. Dividing church activities into programs is difficult, especially dividing the budget by programs. Which program pays the power bill, or how do you equally divide up the expense among programs? So when you are setting up your church's structure, think about how you want to handle the finances.

Growth

Planning for growth is a necessary component in congregational life assessment. We found that most historically black congregations experienced growth since 1995.

In the total sample of black churches, the larger the membership, the more likely growth occurred in the last five years (see figure 5.8 on the following page). Across rural-urban-suburban locations, 56 percent of the congregations with less than one hundred members experienced growth since 1995. Planning for growth should be an aspect of exploration within your congregational life.

Working with Volunteers

Churches benefit from and often depend on a wealth of volunteers. Motivated by faith, volunteers can burn through huge amounts of work with enthusiasm and gusto, work that without the volunteers either would not be done or would have to be done by paid staff. Discussion related to the topic of volunteers is included in this chapter on finances because volunteers are a significant part of maintaining a cost-effective way of operating churches. Volunteers

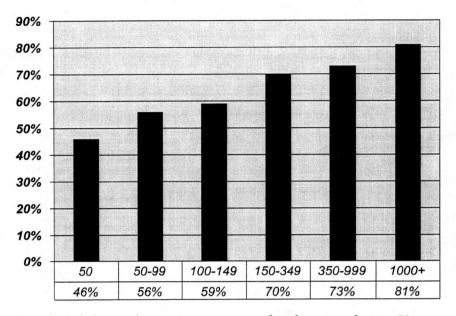

FIGURE 5.8. MEMBERSHIP CHANGE SINCE 1995

50	50-99	100-149	150-349	350-999	1000+
46%	56%	59%	70%	73%	81%

Numbers below columns represent membership size: that is, 50 represents a congregation with 50 members. These data reflect the reported percentage of change in membership between 1995 and 2000.

staff reception desks. They also raise money, gather and prepare food, drive church vans, organize special events, and perform a thousand other important tasks for churches.

Churches are particularly prone to heavy dependence on volunteers for a number of reasons. First, of course, is their faith and the desire to put the tenets of their faith into personal action. Second, funds that run the church come primarily out of the volunteers' pockets. Thus, if it is a choice between hiring a staff person and doing it themselves, volunteers often opt to save money and do the necessary job themselves. At the same time, nearly all churches are understaffed, particularly the small and medium-sized ones. This is a problem, especially in churches where the number of volunteer hours is far greater than the number of paid staff hours each month. The reasons this is a problem are due to two overarching issues related to volunteers: competence and motivation.

Let's go back to the concept of using our gifts from God. Each of us has skills, talents, and abilities with which God has blessed us. This is true for volunteers especially. Some us have the gift of planning, writing, working with children and so on. Additionally, in the last two decades religious congregations have been expected to pick up the slack in governmental services to the needy. Many congregations are eager and willing to do so — and should use their special gifts for the good of others as a good steward of God's different gifts. But this increased use of volunteers in churches raises issues related to managing volunteers. Volunteers are a resource with which God has provided you, and they have to be managed as carefully as you do any other resource. So the first issue with volunteers is managing them wisely.

Try your best to match your volunteer tasks with volunteer skills. This is not always possible because you do not have a bottomless pool of volunteers. They also do not possess expertise in everything you need. But try to match the volunteer to the job. Don't just fill any job with any willing warm body. Further, examine ways in which you can work to make sure they are able and willing to work within your church structure. Because we are people of God, we want to believe the best of our fellow occupants in God's reign on earth. Problems sometimes come after volunteers join the church. We don't have the frameworks for job expectations, evaluation, or discipline in place. Volunteers need to be well-trained and well-informed. Good ways to use volunteers include:

- Recruit volunteers for a task that has a short duration and uses their specific expertise or interest.

- As part of your congregational study, figure out which jobs are appropriate for volunteers to do in your congregation and which are not.

- Be completely forthcoming about the volunteers' obligations. Don't tell them this is a one-time only project when you need someone for the entire year.

- Don't expect to get a lot for nothing.

- Train volunteers. Why? For the same reason you train staff. People have to know what your expectations are of them and who supervises them.

- Evaluation is a tough issue for many churches. The idea of evaluating someone who is giving of their time may seem ridiculous, but think about it from the point of view of your church. You want the best for your church. Evaluation should make sure the volunteer is matched with the job you need. If not, move the volunteer to another job. Volunteers want to help, not hurt, your church, and most will be willing to move to a different task.

- Train your staff how to work with volunteers.

- Say "thank you" often.

- Stay close to your volunteers; often they are the ones who see where your church has a need. Be sure to ask your volunteers about ways to improve the volunteer experience. You won't know what they think until you ask!

Checklist for Chapter 5

- Determining real vs. perceived financial health
- Evaluating financial systems
- Working with volunteers

Questions for Discussion,
Reflection, and Action

1. What does it profit a congregation to raise its budget but lose its mission?

2. What, then, is our mission in the world and in the light of the Christian story? Is it primarily evangelism, primarily justice seeking, primarily charity to the needy, primarily worship, primarily living out the values of the reign of God, or perhaps some combination of these?

3. Is our faith visible enough in our congregation? How do we celebrate our mission? What is the best way to show our mission and the tenets of our faith to the world?

~ Six ~

FINAL THOUGHTS

Now you are the body of Christ and individually members of
it. And God has appointed in the church first apostles, second
prophets, third teachers; then deeds of power, then gifts of
healing, forms of assistance, forms of leadership, various kinds
of tongues. . . . But strive for the greater gifts. And I will show
you a still more excellent way.

— 1 Corinthians 12:27–29, 31

Growth means development in the life of an organism. It
means change manifest in structure. In highly developed organ-
isms such as man, growth means change in structure and
quality of character. Generally it does not mean random development — an irresponsive or irresponsible change.

— Howard Thurman

In the above biblical passage, Paul is speaking to the church at
Corinth. Paul wanted the church members to understand that each
person has spiritual gifts and all gifts are given not for the individual but for the communal advantage. There is a connection between
bringing men and women into a personal relationship with Jesus
Christ and responsible church membership. Life in the congregation is the story of individuals and members as a group who are
discovering and sharing life together and seeking to witness to that
life under God in Jesus Christ. What Paul wanted the church in

Corinth to understand is still essential today: congregations are called to discover and share congregational life for mission in and to the world.

This book is an invitation to a disciplined study of your congregation. It has offered a way to gather information about your congregation and compare that information with a national study of black congregations in the United States.

In this chapter you learn about

- models for a congregational study
- identifying congregational strengths
- developing strategic objectives

Models for Congregational Study

The objective of ITC/FaithFactor Project 2000[1] was to gain a clear and comprehensive understanding of black and predominantly black congregations across the nation. Although that objective was met, the Project 2000 study did not reflect what the findings look like when translated into actual church experience. This book has looked at particular dimensions of congregational life and offered suggestions for comparing a particular congregational profile against the national profile of black congregations. This final chapter offers models by which congregations can participate in the ongoing process of understanding congregational life. Smaller congregations may use the first two models as a means of self-study. The third model illustrates the kind of process that uses a consultant.

Conversation in a Community of Faith: A Process Suggested

Every congregation is a community of faith that consists of individuals and members as a group who are discovering and sharing life together and seeking to witness to their life together under God in Jesus Christ. We offer two models in a process for your congregation to engage in self-evaluation and determine a future they can envision as they seek to fulfill their mission.

A primary objective for the session is to invite leaders of a congregation to enter into conversation about their life as a *worshiping, learning, caring,* and *serving* community. You may also use the process to assist you in finding out how each group or auxiliary thinks of itself and understanding how what it does enables your congregation to fulfill a common mission to which you are committed.

The conversation is designed to extend for no more than ninety minutes. When after ninety minutes it appears that the participants wish to proceed longer, ask them to covenant for no more than thirty additional minutes. These conversations may be extended over two consecutive Saturdays to keep any momentum going. You may also determine what day and time are better in your context. For both of these models, you will need a *facilitator* whose role is to mange the process so that the objectives may be realized. You will also need *moderators.* The general responsibility of the *moderator* is to ensure that discussion is flowing in the group and that the group is on task — exploring and providing answers to the questions, helping to develop the congregation's story, or envisioning possibilities for their future. The *recorder* is to ensure that the main ideas are recorded. It is not important to record detailed answers or complete sentences; it is important to note significant phrases or words that adequately convey some consensus developed. It will be the recorder's responsibility in a subsequent plenary to be the reporter on behalf of the group. The moderator's role is to help the small groups keep on task and ensure that the conversation keeps on track with the objective for your time together. Recorders will keep notes of the salient points in the conversation. These are not so much a verbatim transcript or even minutes of the group conversation as they are a record of themes that emerged in the responses.

Recorders can also serve as *reporters* in the subsequent plenary. The facilitator may be selected or appointed by the pastor or the pastor may fulfill this role. It is our experience that congregations might have persons who function in this role at their jobs. Such a person can be affirmed to give leadership in these exercises on behalf of the community.

Once participants have been invited and the date and time are appointed, the session may proceed as below after gathering and opening rituals:

- The facilitator will share the concept of *congregation as a community of faith*, state the objectives for the session, and explain the process.

- The participants will be divided into groups of no more than six persons.

- Each group will appoint from among its membership one person to *moderate* the discussion and another to *record* its findings for presentation at a subsequent plenary. Moderators and recorders may also be preselected and appointed. Group discussion will extend for forty minutes.

Assignment for Model One

Participants will be asked to engage in the assignment: a conversation on the four understandings of the congregation as a community of faith, as manifested through activities and programs in the areas of *worshiping, caring, learning,* and *serving.*

Assignment for Model Two

Participants will be divided into groups and discuss in each group the questions stated below, using the concept of the congregation as a *worshiping, caring, learning,* and *serving* community.

1. What do we perceive are our accomplishments and strengths?

2. What are those resources that we have — human and material — on which we can draw or rely?

3. What are those things that we passionately care about?

4. What is a vision that we cherish or would like to see for the life of our congregation?

5. What are commitments that we are willing to make, given who we are, what are our strengths are, and what resources we have or are available to us?

Because in model two you are beginning to lay a foundation for program planning, you may need a full hour for group conversations. In either model, the session is brought to closure in a plenary, where recorders share the results of the conversations.

It would be helpful to have an easel pad, either for each group or for use by the facilitator or another person to record answers from the groups. As the reports are received, they may be placed on a wall with masking tape so that all may view the sharing by the several groups. Another value for these postings is that the facilitator, using a different color marker, may highlight similarities or themes from the several groups.

The information gathered in these sessions can lay a foundation for discussion and decision making about goals from which programs can be developed. Through the use of the models your congregation can begin to develop a realistic understanding of itself and develop ministries that are consistent with its self-assessment and its potential for engagement in faithful and obedient ministry.

Model Three: Developing an Assessment in Relation to Other Congregations

To help see how a congregation might participate in a comparative study, we presented a case study of a congregation in the

Atlanta area to examine its personal link between spiritual vitality and demonstrated social outreach. This congregation compared and contrasted data developed through Project 2000 with their particular church experience. The purpose of the study was to

- demonstrate ways in which social outreach was impacted by spiritual vitality; and
- reveal the importance of spirituality to the involvement and impact of congregational social service ministries.

The congregation sought to explore the following:

- Does the denominational and national profile reflect what we know and experience in this congregation?
- What were those items in the national profile that confirm our reality?
- What are those items or situations described that are different, and what is the extent of the difference or variance?

In particular the congregation in this case study wanted to explore the following:

- How does our congregation express its spiritual vitality?
- How does our spiritual vitality impact our social outreach programming?

One of the authors of this book is a member of the congregation involved in this case study. The congregation is in the process of preparing for major physical changes because it has experienced such phenomenal growth during the past decade. Church leaders, pastoral and lay, decided that it was necessary to move to another location in the interest of expansion of all programs within the church. In order to facilitate this move and educate the membership (which totals in the thousands) about the congregation, a case study conducted by one person, rather than a congregational study that included representatives from all programs within the church, was chosen. A report was then made available to the pastor, and all congregational program chairs were directed to begin discussions for an ongoing process of congregational study. The case study included interviews with church staff, lay leaders, volunteers, and community members; observation of church services, outreach programs, meetings, and activities; descriptions of the church's outreach ministries; collection of church documents and budget information; and an assessment of community demographics, needs, and resources.

Part I of the case study examined thirteen categories related to congregational life developed by the ITC/FaithFactor Project 2000 study of black churches. For this case study, both data from the total sample of black churches and United Methodist data provided context for information specific to the congregation being studied. Through information gathered about this particular congregation and comparing it to United Methodist Church (UMC) data and total Project 2000 sample data as illustrated through charts in the following section, a framework was developed for understanding the relationship between spiritual vitality and its impact on congregational social service ministries. Part II of the case study was a further analysis of the characteristics of spiritual vitality and the amount and type of social outreach programs at this United Methodist church. The analysis provided learning about the role that a congregation plays in spiritual and social transformation. The congregation presented in this case study was Cascade United Methodist Church. The case study shows step-by-step how Cascade used the data provided by the ITC/FaithFactor Project 2000 study of black churches to conduct its congregational study. It is a sample of just one way to conduct a congregational study. The previous chapters in this book offered suggestions for additional ways to conduct a study of your congregation. Every congregation will determine a type of study that is most appropriate to their church. But let's see how Cascade UMC conducted a study of their congregation.

Part I of the Cascade Study: Examining and Comparing Data

Distribution of Black Churches by Region in the United States

Over half of the black churches in the total sample, including the UMC denomination, are located in the South. The Methodist denomination in the United States, founded in Georgia in the late 1700s, has a significant proportion of its congregations located in the South. Cascade UMC was established in 1926 in Atlanta, Georgia.

DISTRIBUTION OF BLACK CHURCHES BY REGION

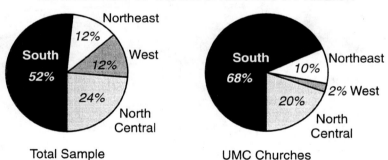

Total Sample   UMC Churches

Distribution of Churches in Rural-Urban Locations

Most of the black churches, including the UMC denomination, are located in urban areas. Cascade UMC is in southwest Atlanta in a first-ring suburban location.

Size of Congregations among Black Churches

Over half of the churches in the total sample of black churches have less than one hundred regularly participating adult members

DISTRIBUTION OF BLACK CHURCHES BY LOCATION

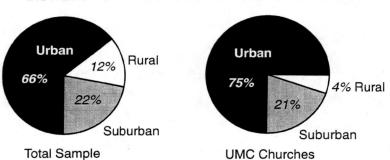

Total Sample   UMC Churches

SIZE OF CONGREGATIONS

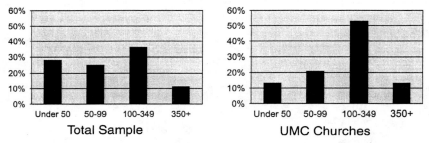

Total Sample   UMC Churches

(28 percent have under fifty members). However, black congregations in the UMC denomination tend to be larger, with less than 30 percent having fewer than a hundred members. Cascade UMC has over five thousand members and is categorized as a megachurch.

Location of Churches of One Hundred or More Active Adult Members

Black churches of one hundred or more active adult members (able to support a full-time pastor) are more likely located in cities and suburbs than in small towns and rural areas. The greatest proportion of these larger churches of the UMC denomination are in suburban and urban areas. Cascade UMC has built larger facilities

SIZE OF CHURCH AND TYPE OF COMMUNITY
Percent of Churches with 100+ Active Members

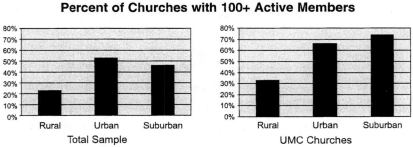

three times and has moved location twice in order to accommodate its growing congregation.

Year Congregation Organized

Over half of the churches in the total sample of black churches were organized before 1945. Few UMC churches have been organized within the last decade. Cascade UMC began in 1926 in a store building and erected its first church structure in 1927. In 1939 it started work on a new building, but work on the new sanctuary was suspended in December 1941 due to World War II. The new sanctuary was completed in 1947 with a seating capacity of 425. Between 1948 and 1954 the church grew so rapidly another sanctuary was

YEAR OF ORGANIZATION

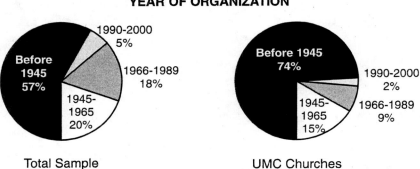

built in 1955, with a church school building and pastorate. But by 1970 the process of racial transition had begun and the congregation began to get smaller. A large portion of the congregation's facilities was sold to the Board of Education in Atlanta. In 1974 a dynamic, young, black minister with proven expertise in transitional church ministry was appointed pastor, and the congregation began to grow again. Cascade UMC outgrew its church building, finding it necessary to hold two morning services and to install television monitors in order to accommodate a growing membership. In 1986 the church found it necessary to begin building again, constructing a "cathedral" to house the current twenty-six hundred members. Cascade UMC is the first predominantly black United Methodist Church to build a structure of this size and magnitude since 1970.

Year Churches Organized in Different Regions

Black churches organized after 1965 are more likely in the western part of the United States. This recent westward expansion in numbers includes the UMC denomination.

CHURCHES BEGUN AFTER 1965, BY REGION

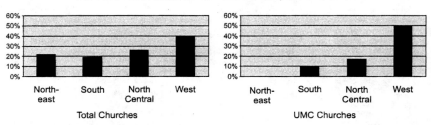

Characteristics of Actively Participating Adults

UMC congregational participants reflect demographic characteristics similar to the total sample of black churches only in the area of

CHARACTERISTICS OF ACTIVE ADULTS

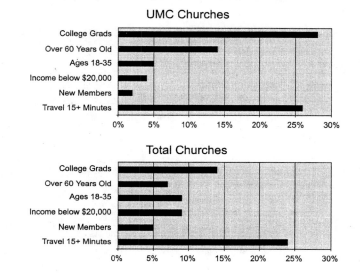

UMC Churches

Total Churches

time to commute. With UMC congregations there is a slight variance in new members, families below $20,000 in annual income, number of congregants between eighteen and thirty-five and over sixty years of age, and number of college graduates.

Distribution of Member Characteristics by Rural-Urban-Suburban Location

Among the three locations, there is significant difference in the presence of college graduates in suburban and urban areas compared to rural areas. Urban churches have slightly higher percentages of persons between eighteen and thirty-five and over sixty years of age. A higher percentage of persons attending UMC churches in urban areas are more likely to commute over fifteen minutes to church, as contrasted with those in rural and suburban areas. Rural congregations have a greater number of new members.

As a suburban church, Cascade UMC holds true to UMC findings with even higher percentages in all areas. Factors that contribute

MEMBER CHARACTERISTICS BY LOCATION

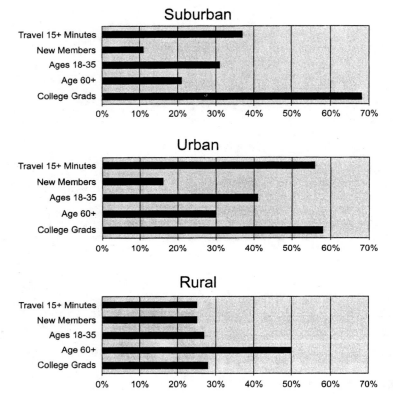

to this include its proximity to the Atlanta University Center, the largest consortium of predominantly black colleges in the nation, the extraordinary economic growth of Atlanta during the last twenty years, and the subsequent phenomenal growth of the black middle and upper-middle class in the Atlanta area.

Distribution of Member Characteristics by Year Church Was Organized

In a comparison of churches established before 1965 and since, the percentage varies significantly in the surveyed items.

MEMBER CHARACTERISTICS
BY YEAR OF ORGANIZATION

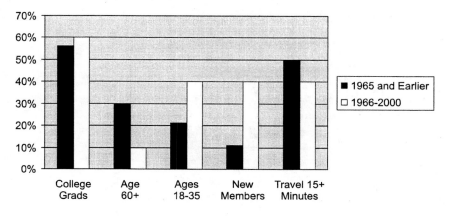

Membership Changes in Black Churches since 1995

A small majority of the black churches, including those of the UMC denomination, have increased at least 5 percent over the last five years. Only a small minority of black churches have decreased 5 percent or more in membership since 1995. Cascade UMC has experienced an extraordinary growth rate of 71 percent since 1994.

Characteristics of Growing Churches

In the total sample of black churches, including the UMC denomination, the larger the membership, the more likely a 5 percent or more growth occurred in the last five years. Reasons for this include:

- Large churches are typically situated in growing population areas.

- Larger churches are better able to have staff and volunteers.

- Larger churches have a wider diversity of programs that engage present members and attract new members.

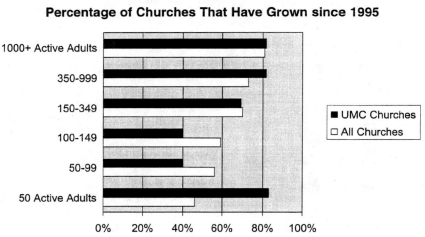

GROWTH IN MEMBERSHIP BY SIZE
Percentage of Churches That Have Grown since 1995

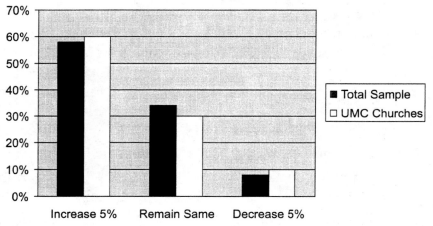

CHARACTERISTICS OF GROWING CHURCHES
Percentage of Growth by Size

Growth and Diversity since 1995

Larger churches offer greater variety of programs to members. However, even in churches of different sizes, the greater the number

GROWTH AND DIVERSITY

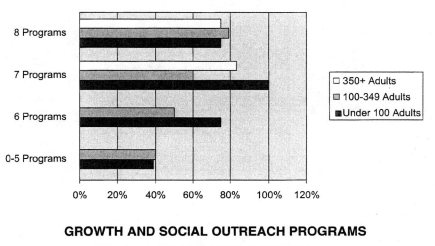

GROWTH AND SOCIAL OUTREACH PROGRAMS

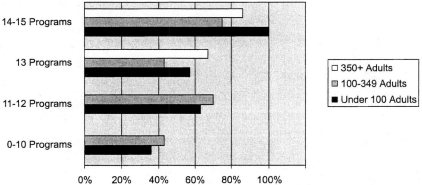

of programs presented to members, the more likely the church has grown in membership since 1995.

Financial Health of Black Churches

A majority of the full sample of black churches surveyed are financially stable. It seems that only a small percentage of black congregations are in serious difficulty. A recent study completed by the Institute of Church Administration and Management located

FINANCIAL HEALTH

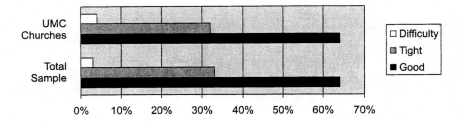

at the Interdenominational Theological Center found the factors most associated with giving in the black church included the church members' age, income, spirituality, religiosity, and how well the church managed its financial affairs. What seemed to motivate black church members to give to their respective houses of worship was their spirituality and commitment to keep God's covenant to support the church.

Commensurate with its extraordinary growth pattern, Cascade UMC has experienced strong financial growth, an average 13 percent increase in giving patterns over the past five years. Several factors contribute to this financial stability: superior record keeping; use of demographic information in fundraising efforts; and a formal stewardship program.

Financial Health, Church Size, and Growth

Larger churches of the UMC denomination are more likely to report being in good financial health than smaller churches. Similarly, churches that have grown 5 percent or more since 1995 are more likely to demonstrate good financial health. Even among growing churches, however, the larger churches still have an advantage. This congregation with its 71 percent growth rate since 1994 exemplifies this Project 2000 finding.

FINANCIAL HEALTH, SIZE, AND GROWTH

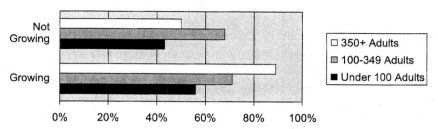

Not Growing

Growing

- □ 350+ Adults
- ▨ 100-349 Adults
- ■ Under 100 Adults

0%   20%   40%   60%   80%   100%

Financial Health and Proportion of Low-Income Families

The financial health of a church depends on its size and financial resources. Churches with a large proportion of adult members with family incomes less than $20,000 a year are significantly less likely to be financially stable than churches with adults with higher incomes. The churches in the best financial health are clearly the larger churches with relatively few low-income families.

PROPORTION OF LOW-INCOME FAMILIES

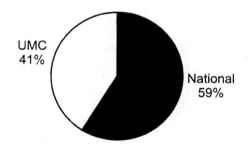

UMC
41%

National
59%

Congregational Life and Vitality

Assimilation of New Persons

The strong majority of churches in the total sample of black churches, including churches of the UMC denomination, do well in assimilating new persons into their life and fellowship. Cascade UMC's 71 percent membership growth rate since 1994 can

ASSIMILATION OF NEW PERSONS

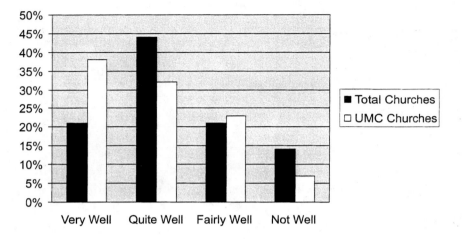

be attributed to two patterns for assimilation. The first pattern relates to its method of assimilating visitors into the fellowship of the church. Greeters are stationed at strategic spots throughout the vestibule to the sanctuary to record names and addresses of all visitors. A member from the congregation reads these names during the worship service while the visitors are asked to stand and be recognized. The entire congregation then sings (while using sign language) a song inviting visitors to be a part of the congregation and ends with communal fellowship that includes greeting visitors and friends with hugs and handshakes.

The second pattern for new member assimilation is a call to join the church at the end of each service. After a public introduction to the congregation, membership committee persons take these new members to a room near the sanctuary to complete general information forms that include signing up for a day-long workshop held each month introducing new members both to the activities available to them and to key persons representing these activities. New members are "assigned" a class name, the class of Mark, the class of Paul and so on. For a period of eight weeks all new members are assigned to a particular "class." The classes have numerous social and church committee activities in which new members are invited to participate and thereby develop a base of friendships and common interests. The developing class acts as "old members" to the new members who are added each week for the eight-week period. A specific area in the sanctuary is set aside for the developing class to sit each week. This allows for a level of familiarity with routines of worship service and each other to solidify assimilation and commitment to the church. At the end of eight weeks, the class "graduates" and participates in a special ceremony honoring their commitment to the church. Often when new members begin participating in specific activities related to worship service, they are cited by the pastor for their involvement.

Assimilation and Program Diversity

The effectiveness with which UMC congregations assimilate new persons and retain them as members is not related to region of the country or rural-urban location. Larger churches have the advantage in offering diversity of programs and of worship experience.

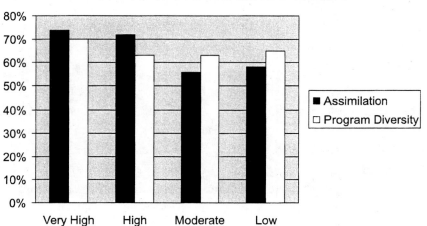

ASSIMILATION AND PROGRAM DIVERSITY

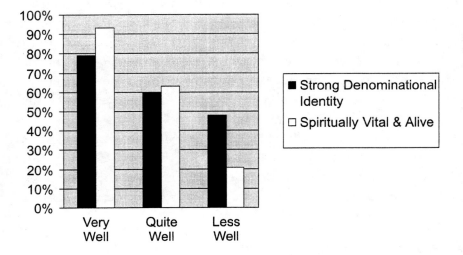

ASSIMILATION AND CHURCH CHARACTERISTICS

However, size is not that important; larger churches are only slightly more likely than smaller churches to incorporate new persons easily. (These charts, like others in this section and elsewhere in the book, when describing the characteristics of multiple variables, are not intended to present percentages that add up to 100.)

Assimilation of New Persons, Denominational Identity, and Church Vitality

UMC congregations that emphasize their heritage and are spiritually vital assimilate newcomers well. A central component of the eight-week assimilation of new members at Cascade UMC is education related to Methodist practices, polity, and theology. Topics covered in new member classes include church data; history of the congregation; ministry divisions; summary of Methodist history; African Americans' United Methodist heritage; summary of United Methodist structure; brief history of Christianity; stewardship; tithing; and baptism. Over half of new persons joining

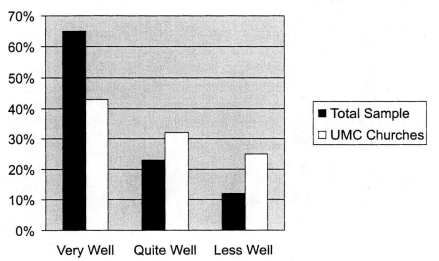

this congregation are from other denominations. Even for those persons transferring membership from another United Methodist church, this educational process is reaffirming, encouraging, and enlightening.

Church Vitality

Almost all leaders of black churches, including those of the UMC denomination, believe being spiritually vital characterizes their congregation.

Spiritual Vitality and Program Diversity

UMC church leaders who view their congregations as spiritually vital are likely to characterize their congregations as

- helping members deepen the relationship to god;
- being excited about the future of their congregation;
- assimilating new members into the life of congregation;

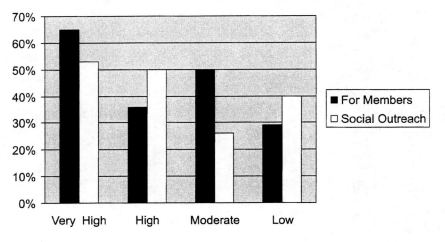

SPIRITUAL VITALITY AND PROGRAM DIVERSITY

- working for social justice; and
- giving expression to denominational heritage.

Diversity of programs contributes to spiritual vitality by attracting new members and involving them in the church. Diversity in types of programs for social outreach contributes to congregational vitality.

Spiritual Vitality and Music

Diversity in music types — that is, spirituals, modern gospel, gospel rap, and dance — enhances congregational spiritual vitality in black churches, including UMC churches. Cascade UMC has five choruses (women's chorus, men's chorus, chancel choir, gospel choir, and contemporary music choir) as well as a classically trained interpretive dancer who performs on special occasions.

Pastoral Leadership and Clergy Education

A small minority of pastors of black churches have a certificate degree or less for ministry. Half attended Bible college or seminary. In the full sample of black churches having a pastor with a

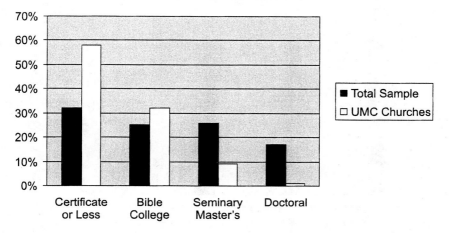

seminary master's degree, nearly a third have continued with formal education for ministry. Pastors of UMC churches are equally well educated. Cascade's pastor and the four associate pastors all have master of divinity degrees. The pastor has also received two honorary doctor of divinity degrees because of his distinguished involvement in evangelism, pastoral care, preaching, and community service.

Education and Size of Church

Education does not directly affect the extent to which pastors report their congregations as being spiritually vital, helping members deepen their relationship to God, being excited about the future, assimilating newcomers, or working for social justice. However, the more education clergy have, the more likely they are to pastor larger congregations.

Women Pastors

In the total sample of black clergy, the better educated the pastors, the more favorable they are toward women pastors. UMC

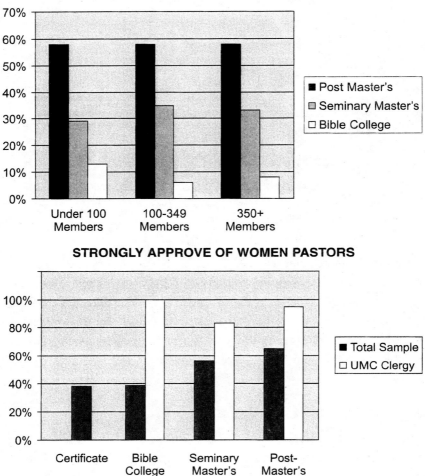

SIZE OF UMC CHURCH AND PASTOR'S EDUCATION

STRONGLY APPROVE OF WOMEN PASTORS

pastors, however, are highly in favor of clergywomen in each level of educational attainment. Cascade UMC's pastor has included a women associate pastor on the staff during both his tenures at this church (1974–1985 and 1992–current). The pastor maintains a policy of sharing the preaching with the women associate pastors on an equal basis.

Protest Marches or Civil Rights Issues

In the total sample of black clergy, those with seminary degrees and particularly doctoral degrees are more likely to approve of clergy being actively involved in political action. UMC clergy, regardless of their educational attainment, on the whole, approve of clergy involvement in protest marches and civil rights issues.

The pastors of Cascade UMC (since 1974) have both been civil rights leaders and active in social justice issues.

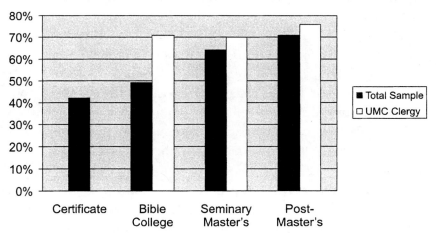

STRONGLY APPROVE OF CLERGY IN PROTEST MARCHES

Analysis of Spiritual Vitality and Social Outreach Programming in the Congregation Being Studied

The black church in the United States has a long history of spiritual vitality and social outreach. Regardless of denomination, black worship has several commonalities:[2]

- praise and thanksgiving to God while being spiritually nourished;

- affirmation of God's providence and power;

- common historical taproot that extends deep into the nurturing center of the African heritage; and

- struggle for survival as African people in America.

From the African taproot came a Christian worldview, or "sacred cosmos," "that permeated every aspect of life."[3] W. E. B. Du Bois was probably the first African American scholar to discern that the origins of African American religious leadership are deeply embedded in traditional African culture.[4] Among freed African Americans, the spirit of African kingship was transmitted to the clergy, whom the community viewed as their primary leaders. From earliest times up to the present, black clergy have been acknowledged as the titular heads of their local communities and have enjoyed the highest respect and loyalty of their people and can be relied upon to care for their material needs.[5] As the only stable and coherent institutional area to emerge from slavery, black churches not only were dominant in their communities, but also became the womb of black culture and a number of major social institutions.[6] Andrew Billingsley, in his study of over eighteen hundred black churches involved in social reform, found that, as a group, Methodist churches are likely to be actively involved in community outreach programs.[7] The following is an examination of Cascade UMC's assessment of church vitality and the role vitality plays in its social outreach programming.

Spiritual Vitality

Before an examination of spiritual vitality can be engendered, a definition of spiritual vitality is required. For the purposes of this study, spiritual vitality includes individuals and communities in a process that involves a liberating encounter, a liberating reflection, and a liberating action.[8] Any discussion of spirituality should start with a note of personal engagement. Additionally, spiritual vitality is greatly enhanced when it is experienced in community with others.[9]

How is spiritual vitality experienced at Cascade UMC? As a liberating encounter, it is initially often experienced through the process of joining the church. The process of joining this congregation becomes a liberating encounter through a deliberate series of activities supported by the church community that leads to active involvement within the church. Included within the activities is strong encouragement for participation in a wide range of biblical studies. These biblical studies provide a "liberating reflection" experience to complete the process cycle defined above.

As a new member, one's initial encounter is through a discipleship ministry whose mission is to nourish the spirit of new members with unconditional love, receiving them with open arms, so that they can help transform the world through unity and be in right relationship with one another and with eternal God. Discipleship ministry work areas include

- *intake* — responsible for intake of new members during all worship services;
- *communications* — responsible for corresponding with new members on a regular basis;
- *orientation* — conducting classes for new members one Saturday each month; current Cascade members function as facilitators or administrators.
- *confirmation* — organization of new members for their new member confirmation service held on the Sunday following the orientation class; and
- *nurture* — outreach to church family via cards, flowers, visits, and phone calls.

During orientation new members are encouraged to identify areas of interest and involvement within the congregation's social action ministries. Focus areas within Cascade UMC include nurture, outreach, witness, and worship.

Nurture activities include

- children's ministries

- Christian education

- church school

- family ministries

- marriage enrichment

- singles ministry

- torchbearers (older adults)

- Good Choices, Inc. (youth banking program)

Outreach activities include

- church and society (Habitat House)

- health and welfare

- higher education (provides a "link" between Cascade and local campuses)

- Girl Scouts

- recreation

- missions

- homeless ministry

- interracial ministry

- resurrection (provides support for families who have experienced death in the family; care for a disabled family member; and care for those suffering from broken relationships or employment problems)

Witness activities include

- caregivers (visitation)
- evangelism
- discipleship
- prayer ministry
- communications
- United Methodist men
- United Methodist women

Worship activities involve:

- music (five choirs)
- ushers
- communion stewards
- lay leaders
- sign ministry
- drama
- confirmation classes (taught by senior pastor)
- celebration of life ministry (bereavement and birth)
- acolytes
- greeters
- weddings

In addition to the above activities, members can participate in a range of activities related to the ongoing operations of the church that include:

- church council
- staff-pastor-parish relations committee
- finance committee

- trustee board
- support services (program management, food services, traffic, bus drivers, custodial staff, nursery staff, security, operations)

The diversity of programs contributes to spiritual vitality by attracting new members and involving them in the life of the church. Annually, the congregation conducts a churchwide "leadership retreat" where over one thousand members participate in the planning of the following year's activities. In the break-out sessions, leaders of particular ministries make reports to the larger focus area leaders. Ministry focus areas are nurture, outreach, witness, and worship.

Each ministry completes a "Ministry Action Plan" for the upcoming year that includes the purpose of the ministry for the next year; identification of "guiding scripture"; a list of activities; how each program will fit into the congregation's annual theme (the theme for 2001 was "Spiritually Transforming the World"); implementation steps; dates and times for program activities; and budget. Additionally, Cascade UMC has adopted a wide rather than narrow definition of the role of political agency in spiritual vitality. Although the congregational leadership does not advocate particular political personages, it does give attention to the concept of the "political" as essential to the notion of spiritual vitality. Church members are encouraged to vote; political leaders are invited and honored in church services; and church members are encouraged to express their spiritual empowerment through political empowerment, all within the rubric of "being a light in the community."

Congregational Social Service Ministries

Diversity in the types of programs for social outreach contributes to congregational vitality. The black church has a unique history of being the single most important institution embodying goals and purposes that pertain primarily to the welfare of black people. That uniqueness is significant because in the United States there have been no other enduring institutions with such purposes.[10]

Cascade UMC has a significant history of community social outreach programs. For example, it has participated in a community outreach fund for over thirty years. On the first Sunday of each month, funds are collected during all worship services (three services) for the Community Outreach Fund. One hundred percent of the funds collected are distributed for identified immediate needs. For two hours on the Tuesday following Community Fund Sunday, eight to ten staff members participate in a "hotline" answering requests for emergency financial assistance from both members of the congregation and the larger Atlanta community, although requests from the larger community far outnumber requests from the congregation. Areas of assistance include mortgages, rent, and utilities. Assistance also consists of counseling and financial management advice. Cascade UMC is a referral organization for the United Way, Salvation Army, St. Vincent De Paul, and several local social service agencies and processes over seventy requests each month.

Traditionally at the end of most Protestant church services, a benediction or blessing is pronounced. The benediction is oriented toward the people in the congregation and "blesses" them and the work they do. The blessing is the end of the worship service. At Cascade UMC there is no blessing at the end of worship service. Instead there is a ritual of "sending forth" that has developed into a tradition. This tradition is specifically designed to communicate a commitment to social outreach. In the "sending forth" all members of the congregation are encouraged and expected to be involved in outreach activities. This encouragement is intentional and based on the model of Christ "sending disciples out two by two" to work in the world. At Cascade UMC, when you leave the physical church sanctuary, you are going out "being the church." The ceremony of sending forth consists of three components: (1) joining hands, symbolizing connection and that one is not by oneself in the work of community outreach; (2) movement, symbolizing rhythm and that reaching out and being involved in outreach should be a part of the rhythm of one's life rather than just an activity; and (3) song based on scripture, Philippians 4:13, "We can do all things [in] Christ who strengthens us." At the end of the chant, hands are raised, symbolizing that we are being sent out on a "positive note." We *can* do *all* things *in* Christ who strengthens us.

Often social outreach programs sponsored by churches focus on immediate needs. Although Cascade UMC has numerous outreach ministries with this type of orientation (see above list of outreach activities), it also has incorporated a "futurist mentality" into several outreach programs. Examples include a focus on higher education.

Higher Education Ministry and Interracial Relations Ministry

Cascade UMC has also established a scholarship and awards budget to assist members and individuals in pursuing higher education. Since 1984, it has provided scholarships in excess of a quarter million dollars. In conjunction with this scholarship program, Cascade UMC has established an "Incentive Award" that is given to two students at a local high school who have participated in and have been leaders of social outreach programs within a local low-income community in southwest Atlanta. Additionally, the higher education ministry provides assistance to outreach groups interested in developing higher education/campus ministry programs. Other activities include workshops; middle-school educational resources for high school courses that are prerequisites for college or university studies; Atlanta University Center (AUC) campus ministry program; an ecumenical symposium; bus service to worship services each Sunday from the AUC campus; a student loan program; and a grant fund.

The interracial ministry was created to overcome the paralysis and inaction often resulting from the effects of racism. Three components of this ministry include (1) collaboration with a local white church in annually constructing a Habitat for Humanity home; (2) a "friend-to-friend" program that connects a single adult from the congregation with another single adult from local UM churches in Atlanta: both "friends" commit to building a cross-racial friendship that includes regular meals, activities, and worship for an extended period of time; and a young adult program of planned activities with a predominantly white congregation within the UMC.

Making Fundamental Decisions for the Future

The congregational study above is an example of one way to examine a congregation to help with decisions for the future. This congregation was facing a wide range of changes it needed to make in order to meet the needs of persons within its surrounding community and within its specific church community. In order to engage a large number of persons into the process of making fundamental decision for its future, it decided to use a study of its congregation that was conducted by a professional who was a member of the church and trained in congregational studies. The study and its method were to give readers an example of the kind of disciplined study in which larger congregations can engage, using a trained consultant. The study covered all the areas of a congregation's life that we have discussed in chapters 2 through 5.

Identifying Congregational Strengths

No one measure is definitive for identifying the strength of congregational life. One can only present a small number of indicators from a range of measures of congregational strength.

One set of measures was chosen for the study that developed the national profile reported by Faith Communities Today. The six areas of focus chosen were: public worship, spiritual growth, inviting and including, community outreach, managing and leading, and finances. In an alternative focus, we have given attention in this book to the following areas in the ITC/FaithFactor Project 2000: worship and identity; facilities; internal and mission-oriented programs; leadership and organizational dynamics; and finances.

In this chapter we have offered models for assessing congregational life. Your congregation may use the two models for self-evaluation, using skilled persons identified from within the congregation. You are invited to examine your congregation as a worshiping, caring, learning, and serving community. In these models congregations are asked a fundamental question: How do you see yourselves in these areas, identifying your strengths and challenges (rather than weaknesses) — areas in which improvement is suggested. The other and more extensive study requires a consultant.

Whichever model or process is used, the following general questions may be framed to evoke answers about strengths or challenges. These include:

- How do you understand your *mission* (purpose) as people of God and how faithful and obedient are you to that mission?

- What is the level of *participation* of the total membership? Is there a place where persons have a sense of *belonging* and involvement in the community, where their gifts are celebrated and used and they are affirmed?

- How does the *leadership* assist in sharing the responsibility for fulfilling the congregation's mission as people of God?

In summary, we can group this concern for strengths under the following broad headings: leadership, purpose (mission), faith development or nurture, disciple making and sending, and strong sense of community and belonging.

Developing Strategic Objectives

We have consistently proposed in this book that congregations need to become self-aware in every area of their lives. But self-awareness and self-knowledge are of little or no value unless they help you to maintain a lifestyle that is consistent with high standards or values that you hold. Congregational life is shaped in similar ways. But things don't just happen: they must be imagined and planned and strategies must be developed to make them happen. We hope that we have provided you with data from a national profile that will help you to examine your own congregation and lead you to ask your own questions in self-examination. We trust that the illustrations we have offered suggest some ways you may shape or reshape your congregation's life, and we hope we have shared some resources or pointed you to others who may assist you as you commit yourself and your congregation to be used by God in God's work in the world.

We are completing this book in the season of Pentecost. The coming of the Spirit as described in the scriptures is identified with the flow of our Christian life and as fulfillment of the promise that Jesus made to his disciples. In a real sense, the coming of the Spirit cannot be limited to any particular period in history. It is a recurring and dynamic reality. The Spirit's dynamism (*dunamis* is the Greek word for power used in Acts 2) is present in every congregation. It is poured out upon the whole world at every moment in every living thing. It is that which gives life to a congregation. Without the free flowing of the Spirit, we would as individuals and as congregations be spiritual asthmatics, gasping for breath — the breath of life. It is by the Spirit that we have life and life is sustained and shaped for the future.

Checklist for Chapter 6

- Determine a model you may use and plan for a study of your congregation.

- Develop a list of strengths that you have observed in the life of your congregation.

- Design and carry out a session to discuss and develop strategies for your future as a congregation.

Questions for Discussion, Reflection, and Action

1. How does our congregation explore the ways that we engage in ministry through community, worship, and social mission?

2. What dynamics knit our congregation together? How does communication occur? How are problems solved and conflicts managed?

3. What areas in our congregational life can we identify as strengths, and why?

4. In what ways does our congregation maintain its spiritual vitality?

~ *Appendix A* ~

FACT DENOMINATIONS
AND FAITH GROUPS

American Baptist Churches USA

Assemblies of God

Baha'is of the United States

Christian Church (Disciples of Christ)

Christian Reformed Church

Churches of Christ (Non-Instrumental)

Church of Jesus Christ of Latter-day Saints

Church of the Nazarene

Episcopal Church

Evangelical Lutheran Church in America

Historically Black Denominations

    African Methodist Episcopal Church

    African Methodist Episcopal Zion Church

    Christian Methodist Episcopal Church

    Church of God in Christ

    National Baptist Convention of America

    National Baptist Convention U.S.A.

    Progressive National Baptist Convention

Independent Christian Church (Instrumental)

Islam

Judaism

   Conservative Judaism

   Reform Judaism

Megachurches

Mennonite Church USA

Nondenominational Groups

Orthodox Christian Groups

     Albanian Orthodox Diocese of America

     American Carpatho-Russian Orthodox Greek Catholic
       Diocese

     Antiochian Orthodox Christian Archdiocese of North America

     Bulgarian Eastern Orthodox Church

     Greek Orthodox Archdiocese of America

     Orthodox Church in America

     Romanian Orthodox Archdiocese in America and Canada

     Serbian Orthodox Church in America

     Ukrainian Orthodox Church of the U.S.A.

Presbyterian Church (USA)

Reformed Church in America

Roman Catholic Church

Seventh-Day Adventist Church

Southern Baptist Convention

Unitarian Universalist Association

United Church of Christ

United Methodist Church

~ *Appendix B* ~

DENOMINATIONAL CHARTS OF RURAL-URBAN-SUBURBAN LOCATIONS

AME Distribution of Member Characteristics (Rural)

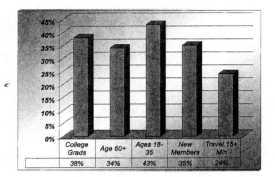

	College Grads	Age 60+	Ages 18-35	New Members	Travel 15+ Min
	38%	34%	43%	35%	24%

AME Distribution of Member Characteristics (Urban)

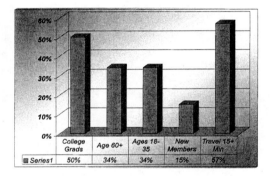

	College Grads	Age 60+	Ages 18-35	New Members	Travel 15+ Min
Series1	50%	34%	34%	15%	57%

AME Distribution of Member Characteristics (Suburban)

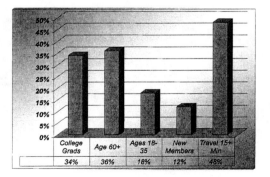

	College Grads	Age 60+	Ages 18-35	New Members	Travel 15+ Min
	34%	36%	18%	12%	48%

AMEZ Distribution of Member Characteristics (Rural)

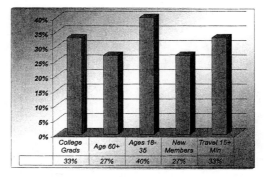

	College Grads	Age 60+	Ages 18-35	New Members	Travel 15+ Min
	33%	27%	40%	27%	33%

AMEZ Distribution of Member Characteristics (Urban)

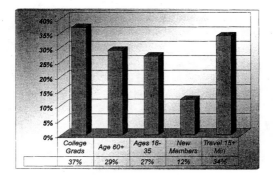

	College Grads	Age 60+	Ages 18-35	New Members	Travel 15+ Min
	37%	29%	27%	12%	34%

AMEZ Distribution of Member Characteristics (Suburban)

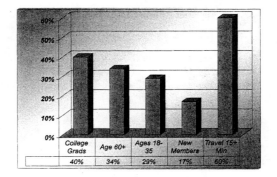

	College Grads	Age 60+	Ages 18-35	New Members	Travel 15+ Min
	40%	34%	29%	17%	60%

Baptist Distribution of Member Characteristics (Rural)

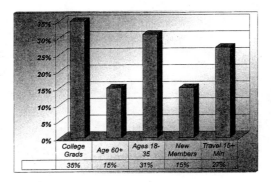

	College Grads	Age 60+	Ages 18-35	New Members	Travel 15+ Min
	35%	15%	31%	15%	27%

Baptist Distribution of Member Characteristics (Urban)

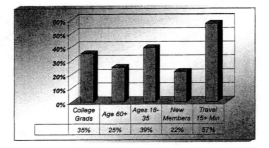

	College Grads	Age 60+	Ages 18-35	New Members	Travel 15+ Min
	35%	25%	39%	22%	57%

Baptist Distribution of Member Characteristics (Suburban)

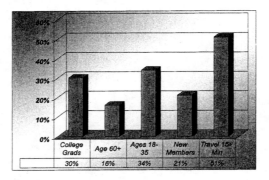

	College Grads	Age 60+	Ages 18-35	New Members	Travel 15+ Min
	30%	16%	34%	21%	51%

CME Distribution of Member Characteristics (Rural))

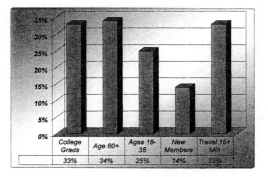

College Grads	Age 60+	Ages 18-35	New Members	Travel 15+ Min
33%	34%	25%	14%	33%

CME Distribution of Member Characteristics (Urban)

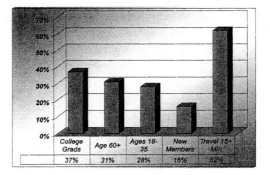

College Grads	Age 60+	Ages 18-35	New Members	Travel 15+ Min
37%	31%	28%	16%	62%

CME Distribution of Member Characteristics (Suburban)

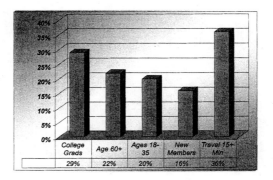

College Grads	Age 60+	Ages 18-35	New Members	Travel 15+ Min
29%	22%	20%	16%	36%

COGIC Distribution of Member Characteristics (Rural)

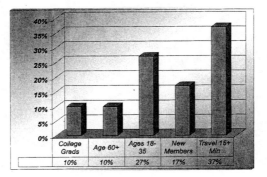

	College Grads	Age 60+	Ages 18-35	New Members	Travel 15+ Min
	10%	10%	27%	17%	37%

COGIC Distribution of Member Characteristics (Urban)

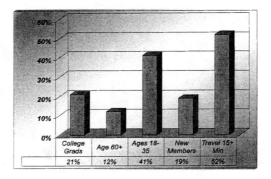

	College Grads	Age 60+	Ages 18-35	New Members	Travel 15+ Min
	21%	12%	41%	19%	52%

COGIC Distribution of Member Characteristics (Suburban)

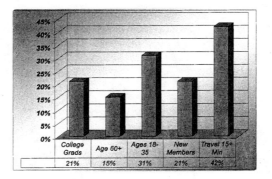

	College Grads	Age 60+	Ages 18-35	New Members	Travel 15+ Min
	21%	15%	31%	21%	42%

Presbyterian Distribution of Member Characteristics (Rural)

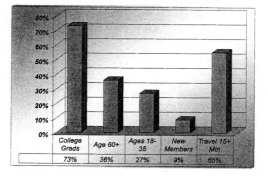

	College Grads	Age 60+	Ages 18-35	New Members	Travel 15+ Min
	73%	36%	27%	9%	55%

Presbyterian Distribution of Member Characteristics (Urban)

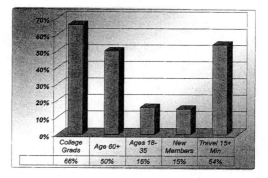

	College Grads	Age 60+	Ages 18-35	New Members	Travel 15+ Min
	66%	50%	16%	15%	54%

Presbyterian Distribution of Member Characteristics (Suburban)

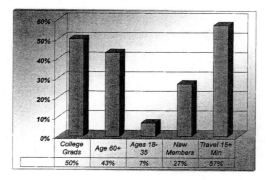

	College Grads	Age 60+	Ages 18-35	New Members	Travel 15+ Min
	50%	43%	7%	27%	57%

UMC Distribution of Member Characteristics (Rural)

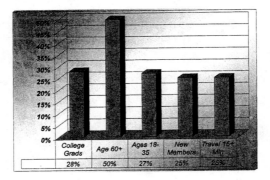

	College Grads	Age 60+	Ages 18-35	New Members	Travel 15+ Min
	28%	50%	27%	25%	25%

UMC Distribution of Member Characteristics (Urban)

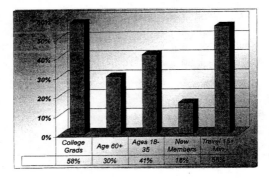

	College Grads	Age 60+	Ages 18-35	New Members	Travel 15+ Min
	58%	30%	41%	18%	55%

UMC Distribution of Member Characteristics (Suburban)

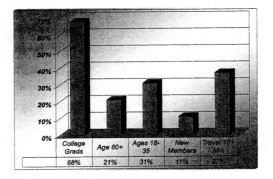

	College Grads	Age 60+	Ages 18-35	New Members	Travel 15+ Min
	68%	21%	31%	11%	37%

NOTES

Introduction

1. See John S. Mbiti, *Concepts of God in Africa* (New York: Praeger, 1970), chaps. 8–13.

2. Cited in "Jesse Takes Up the Collection," in *Time,* February 6, 1984, 57.

3. Gallup Organization, *ITC/FaithFactor Project 2000 Final Research Report* (2000), 6.

4. Carl S. Dudley and David A. Roozen, *Faith Communities Today: A Report on Religion in the United States Today* (Hartford, Conn.: Hartford Institute for Religious Research, Hartford Seminary, 2001), 4.

5. Melva Wilson Costen, *African American Christian Worship* (Nashville: Abingdon, 1993), 21.

6. George Gallup Jr. and D. Michael Lindsay, *Surveying the Religious Landscape: Trends in U.S. Beliefs* (Harrisburg, Pa.: Morehouse, 1999), 9.

7. Nancy T. Ammerman, *Congregation and Community* (New Brunswick, N.J.: Rutgers University Press, 1997).

8. Andrew Billingsley, *Mighty Like a River* (New York: Oxford University Press, 1999), 185.

Chapter 1

1. D. T. Niles, *The Preacher's Calling to Be Servant* (London: Lutterworth, 1959), 29.

2. William D. Watley is pastor of St. James AME Church in Newark, New Jersey. The story was included in "Theological Linguistics," an address delivered at Hampton University Ministers' Conference, Hampton, Va., June 7, 2000.

3. Nancy T. Ammerman et al., *Studying Congregations: A New Handbook* (Nashville: Abingdon, 1998), 78.

4. Carl S. Dudley and David A. Roozen, *Faith Communities Today: A Report on Religion in the United States Today* (Hartford, Conn.: Hartford Institute for Religious Research, Hartford Seminary, 2001), 17.

5. Andrew Greeley, *The Denominational Society: A Sociological Approach to Religion in America* (Glenview, Ill.: Scott, Foresman and Company, 1972).

6. Thomas Moore, *Soul Mates: Honoring the Mysteries of Love and Relationships* (New York: HarperPerennial, 1994), 120.

7. Gustavo Gutiérrez, *On Job: God-Talk and the Suffering of the Innocent* (Maryknoll, N.Y.: Orbis Books, 1987), xviii.

8. William B. McClain, "What Is Authentic Black Worship?" in *Experiences, Struggles, and Hopes of the Black Church,* ed. James S. Gadsen (Nashville: Discipleship Resources — Tidings, 1974), 69.

9. Gallup Organization, *ITC/FaithFactor Project 2000 Final Research Report* (2000), 16.

10. Mellonee V. Burnim, "Religious Music," in *The Garland Encyclopedia of World Music,* vol. 3: *The United States and Canada,* ed. Ellen Koskoff (New York: Garland, 2001), 624. See also Mellonee V. Burnim and Portia K. Maultsby, "From Backwoods to City Streets: The Afro-American Musical Journey," in *Expressively Black,* ed. Geneva Gay and Willie L. Barber (New York: Praeger, 1987).

11. Gallup Organization, *ITC/FaithFactor Project 2000,* 55.

12. Ibid., 16.

13. Melva Wilson Costen, "African-American Worship: Faith Looking Forward," *Journal of the Interdenominational Theological Center* 27 (fall 1999–spring 2000): 1.

14. *Hymns and Songs: A Supplement to the Methodist Hymn Book* (London: Methodist Publishing House, 1969), 97.

15. Gallup Organization, *ITC/FaithFactor Project 2000,* 25.

16. Dr. Melody T. McCloud, who is the lead author of *Blessed Health: The African American Woman's Guide to Physical and Spiritual Well-Being* (Simon & Schuster, 2003), shared this poem in conversation with one of us. A version of the poem was previously published in the *Atlanta Journal-Constitution,* March 9, 2003, B2.

17. Dudley and Roozen, *Faith Communities Today,* 32.

18. George B. Thompson Jr., *How to Get Along with Your Church: Creating Cultural Capital for Doing Ministry* (Cleveland: Pilgrim, 2001), 28.

19. Sobonfu Somé, *The Spirit of Intimacy: Ancient African Teachings in the Ways of Relationships* (New York: William Morrow, 1999), 22.

Chapter 2

1. John N. Vaughan and Edythe Draper, eds., *The Almanac of the Christian World 1993–94* (Wheaton, Ill.: Tyndale House, 1992).

2. Frank S. Mead, *Handbook of Denominations in the United States,* 10th ed. (Nashville: Abingdon, 1995), 53, 114, 199–200, 204.

3. Nancy L. Eiesland and R. Stephen Warner, "Ecology: Seeing the Congregation in Context," in *Studying Congregations,* ed. Nancy T. Ammerman et al. (Nashville: Abingdon Press, 1998), 40–77.

4. Thomas Luckman, *The Invisible Religion: The Problem of Religion in Modern Society* (New York: Macmillan, 1967), 52–54.

5. Melva Wilson Costen, *African American Christian Worship* (Nashville: Abingdon, 1993), 15.

6. Eiesland and Warner, "Ecology," 48.

7. Barbara R. Rowe, George W. Haynes, and Kathryn Stafford, "The Contributions of Home-Based Business Income to Rural and Urban Economics," *Economic Development Quarterly* 13 (February 1999).

8. C. Eric Lincoln and Lawrence H. Mamiya, *The Black Church in the African American Experience* (Durham, N.C.: Duke University Press, 1990), 384.

9. Carl S. Dudley, *Making the Small Church Effective* (Nashville: Abingdon, 1978), 178.

10. Rupe Simms, "Christ Is Black with a Capital B: An African-American Christianity and the Black Studies Project," in *The Western Journal of Black Studies* 24 (2000): 103.

11. Ibid., 104.

12. W. E. B. Du Bois, *The Souls of Black Folk* (New York: Penguin, 1989), 157.

13. Booker T. Washington, *The Story of the Negro: The Rise of the Race from Slavery* (Gloucester, Mass.: P. Smith, 1969).

14. Milton Sernett, ed., *Afro-American Religious History* (Durham, N.C.: Duke University Press, 1985), 5.

15. Gayraud S. Wilmore, *Black Religion and Black Radicalism,* 3d ed. (Maryknoll, N.Y.: Orbis Books, 1998), 253.

16. Robert M. Franklin, *Another Day's Journey: Black Churches Confronting the American Crisis* (Minneapolis: Augsburg Fortress, 1997), 53.

17. See Lincoln and Mamiya, *The Black Church in the African American Experience,* 8.

Chapter 3

1. Barry White, "Practice What You Preach," in *Barry White: The Ultimate Collection* (New York: Universal Music Studios East, 2000).

2. Gallup Organization, *ITC/FaithFactor Project 2000 Final Research Report* (2000), 43.

3. James A. Forbes Jr., "Social Transformation," in *Living with Apocalypse: Spiritual Resources for Social Compassion,* ed. Tilden Edwards (San Francisco: Harper and Row, 1984), 41.

4. James Baldwin, "White Racism or World Community?" in *Ecumenical Review* 20 (October 1968): 376.

5. Norman Jordan, "I Have Seen Them," in *New Black Voices,* ed. Abraham Chapman (New York: New American Library, 1972).

6. Gallup Organization, *ITC/FaithFactor Project 2000,* 46.

7. Carl S. Dudley and David A. Roozen, *Faith Communities Today: A Report on Religion in the United States Today* (Hartford, Conn.: Hartford Institute for Religious Research, Hartford Seminary, 2001), 48.

8. Ibid., 49.

9. C. Eric Lincoln and Lawrence H. Mamiya, *The Black Church in the African American Experience* (Durham, N.C.: Duke University Press, 1990), 203.

10. Ibid., 234.

Chapter 4

1. Jarena Lee, "My Call to Preach," in *Spiritual Narratives* (New York: Oxford University Press, 1988), 10.

2. Terry D. Anderson, *Transforming Leadership: New Skills for an Extraordinary Future* (Amherst, Mass.: Human Resource Development Press, 1992), 72.

3. Michael I. N. Dash, Stephen C. Rasor, and Christine D. Chapman, *ITC/FaithFactor Project 2000 Study of Black Churches* (Atlanta: Interdenominational Theological Center, 2001).

4. Carl S. Dudley and David A. Roozen, *Faith Communities Today: A Report on Religion in the United States Today* (Hartford, Conn.: Hartford Institute for Religious Research, Hartford Seminary, 2001), 65.

5. Gallup Organization, *ITC/FaithFactor Project 2000 Final Research Report* (2000), 56.

6. Lee, "My Call to Preach," 11.

7. Black Women in Church and Society is a program at the Interdenominational Theological Center with local and national focuses, seeking to enhance the participation and function of women in church and society.

8. Reverend Gina M. Stewart is pastor of Christ Missionary Baptist Church in Memphis, Tennessee. She shared her story with us when she visited for an interview as a candidate for matriculation in the doctor of ministry program at Interdenominational Theological Center. It is included with her permission.

9. Dash, Rasor, and Chapman, *ITC/FaithFactor Project 2000 Study of Black Churches.*

10. Cheryl Townsend Gilkes, *If It Wasn't for Women . . . : Black Women's Experience and Womanist Culture in Church and Community* (Maryknoll, N.Y.: Orbis Books, 2001), 7.

11. Delores C. Carpenter, *A Time for Honor: A Portrait of African American Clergywomen* (St. Louis: Chalice, 2001).

Chapter 5

1. For recent reflections by a Christian psychologist, see David G. Bennet, *Money Madness and Financial Freedom* (Calgary: Detselig, 1996).

2. "Is Tithing God's Plan?" *Christian Century* 1 (December 1927): 1415–16.

3. The following are two tithing questions from the Project 2000 survey: "Do members of your congregation tithe?" and "What is the percentage of tithers in your congregation?"

Chapter 6

1. Michael I. N. Dash, Stephen C. Rasor, and Christine D. Chapman, *ITC/FaithFactor Project Study 2000 of Black Churches* (Atlanta: Interdenominational Theological Center, 2001).

2. Melva Wilson Costen, *African American Christian Worship* (Nashville: Abingdon, 1993), 13.

3. Thomas Luckman, *The Invisible Religion: The Problem of Religion in Modern Society* (New York: Macmillan, 1967), 52–54.

4. W. E. B. Du Bois, *The Negro Church* (Atlanta: Atlanta University Press, 1903).

5. Peter J. Paris, *The Spirituality of African Peoples* (Minneapolis: Fortress, 1995)

6. C. Eric Lincoln and Lawrence H. Mamiya, *The Black Church in the African American Experience* (Durham, N.C.: Duke University Press, 1990).

7. Andrew Billingsley, *Mighty Like a River: The Black Church and Social Reform* (New York: Oxford University Press, 1999).

8. Michael I. N. Dash, Jonathan Jackson, and Stephen C. Rasor, *Hidden Wholeness: An African American Spirituality for Individuals and Communities* (Cleveland: United Church Press, 1997).

9. Edward P. Wimberly, *Recalling Our Own Stories* (San Francisco: Jossey-Bass, 1997).

10. Peter J. Paris, *The Social Teaching of the Black Churches* (Philadelphia: Fortress, 1982), 9.

BIBLIOGRAPHY

Ammerman, Nancy T. *Congregation and Community*. New Brunswick, N.J.: Rutgers University Press, 1997.

Ammerman, Nancy T., et al. *Studying Congregations: A New Handbook*. Nashville: Abingdon, 1998.

Anderson, Terry D. *Transforming Leadership: New Skills for an Extraordinary Future*. Amherst, Mass.: Human Resource Development Press, 1992.

Barna, George. *The Power of Vision: How You Can Capture and Apply God's Vision for Your Ministry*. Ventura, Calif.: Regal Books, 1992.

Becker, Penny Edgell. *Congregations in Conflict: Cultural Model of Local Religious Life*. New York: Cambridge University Press, 1999.

Billingsley, Andrew H. *Mighty Like a River: The Black Church and Social Reform*. New York: Oxford University Press, 1999.

Callahan, Kennon R. *A New Beginning for Pastors and Congregations: Building an Excellent Match on Your Shared Strengths*. San Francisco: Jossey-Bass, 1999.

Carpenter, Delores C. *A Time for Honor: A Portrait of African American Clergywomen*. St. Louis: Chalice Press, 2001.

Carroll, Jackson W. *Mainline to the Future: Congregations for the Twenty-First Century*. Louisville: Westminster John Knox Press, 2000.

Christiansen, Michael J., ed. *Equipping the Saints: Mobilizing Laity for Ministry*. Nashville: Abingdon, 2000.

Costen, Melva Wilson. *African American Christian Worship*. Nashville: Abingdon, 1993.

Dudley, Carl S., and David A. Roozen. *Faith Communities Today: A Report on Religion in the United States Today*. Hartford, Conn.: Hartford Institute for Religious Research, Hartford Seminary, 2001.

Dudley, Carl S., and Nancy T. Ammerman. *Congregations in Transition: A Guide for Analyzing, Assessing, and Adapting to Changing Communities*. San Francisco: Jossey-Bass, 2002.

Foster, Charles R. *The Future of Christian Education: Educating Congregations*. Nashville: Abingdon, 1994.

Frank, Thomas Edward. *The Soul of the Congregation: An Invitation to Congregational Reflection*. Nashville: Abingdon, 2000.

183

Franklin, Robert M. *Another Day's Journey: Black Churches Confronting the American Crisis*. Minneapolis: Augsburg Fortress, 1997.

Gallup, George, Jr., and D. Michael Lindsay. *Surveying the Religious Landscape: Trends in U.S. Beliefs*. Harrisburg, Pa.: Morehouse, 1999.

Gilkes, Cheryl Townsend. *If It Wasn't for Women . . . : Black Women's Experience and Womanist Culture in Church and Community*. Maryknoll, N.Y.: Orbis Books, 2001.

Harris, James H. *Black Ministers and Laity in the Urban Church: An Analysis of Political and Social Expectations*. Lanham, Md.: University Press of America, 1987.

Hartman, Warren J. *Five Audiences: Identifying Groups in Your Church*. Nashville: Abingdon, 1987.

Herrington, Jim, Mike Bonem, and James H. Furr. *Leading Congregational Change: A Practical Guide for the Transformational Journey*. San Francisco: Jossey-Bass, 2000.

Job, Reuben P. *Spiritual Life in the Congregation: A Guide for Retreats*. Nashville: Upper Room, 1997.

Johnson, Douglas W. *Empowering Leadership Series: Empowering Lay Volunteers*. Nashville: Abingdon, 1991.

Kallestad, Walt. *Turn Your Church Inside Out: Building a Community for Others*. Minneapolis: Fortress, 2000.

Lassiter, Valentino. *Martin Luther King in the African American Preaching Tradition*. Cleveland: Pilgrim, 2001.

Levan, Christopher. *Living in the Maybe: A Steward Confronts the Spirit of Fundamentalism*. Grand Rapids, Mich.: Eerdmans, 1998.

Lincoln, C. Eric, and Lawrence H. Mamiya. *The Black Church in the African American Experience*. Durham, N.C.: Duke University Press, 1990.

Mbiti, John S. *Concepts of God in Africa*. New York: Praeger, 1970.

McKenzie, Vashti M. *Not without a Struggle: Leadership Development for African American Women in Ministry*. Cleveland: United Church Press, 1996.

Mead, Loren B. *Transforming Congregations for the Future*. New York: Alban Institute, 1994.

Miller, Donald E. *Reinventing American Protestantism: Christianity in the New Millennium*. Berkeley: University of California Press, 1999.

Nessan, Craig L. *Beyond Maintenance to Mission: A Theology of the Congregation*. Minneapolis: Fortress, 1999.

Olson, Mark A. *Moving beyond Church Growth: An Alternative Vision for Congregations*. Minneapolis: Fortress, 2000.

Oswald, Robert M., and Robert E. Friedrich. *Discerning Your Congregation's Future: A Strategic and Spiritual Approach*. New York: Alban Institute, 1990.

Paris, Peter J. *The Social Teaching of the Black Churches.* Philadelphia: Fortress, 1982.

———. *The Spirituality of African Peoples.* Minneapolis: Fortress, 1995.

Rabey, Steve. *In Search of Authentic Faith: How Emerging Generations Are Transforming the Church.* Colorado Springs: Waterbrook, 2001.

Schaller, Lyle E. *Getting Things Done: Concepts and Skills for Leaders.* Nashville: Abingdon, 1986.

———. *Innovations in Ministry: Models for the Twenty-First Century.* Nashville: Abingdon, 1994.

Sernett, Milton, ed. *Afro-American Religious History.* Durham, N.C.: Duke University Press, 1985.

Stewart, Carlyle Fielding, III. *The Empowerment Church: Speaking a New Language for Church Growth.* Nashville: Abingdon, 2001.

Tennyson, Mack. *Church Finances for People Who Count.* Grand Rapids, Mich.: Zondervan, 1990.

Thompson, George B., Jr. *How to Get Along with Your Church: Creating Cultural Capital for Doing Ministry.* Cleveland: Pilgrim, 2001.

Wallis, Jim. *Faith Works: Lessons from an Activist Preacher.* New York: Random House, 2000.

Wilkes, Paul. *Excellent Protestant Congregations: The Guide to Best Places and Practices.* Louisville: Westminster John Knox, 2000.

Wilmore, Gayraud S. *Black Religion and Black Radicalism.* 3d ed. Maryknoll, N.Y.: Orbis Books, 1998.

Wimberly, Edward P. *Recalling Our Own Stories: Spiritual Resources for Pastoral Caregivers.* San Francisco: Jossey-Bass, 1997.

INDEX

Numbers in *bold italics* indicate figures.

187